Picture Yourself Cooking with Your Kids

Beth Sheresh

Course Technology PTR

A part of Cengage Learning

COURSE TECHNOLOGY
CENGAGE Learning™

Australia • Brazil • Japan • Korea • Mexico • Singapore • Spain • United Kingdom • United States

COURSE TECHNOLOGY
CENGAGE Learning

**Picture Yourself
Cooking with Your Kids**

Beth Sheresh

**Publisher and General Manager,
Course Technology PTR:**
Stacy L. Hiquet

Associate Director of Marketing:
Sarah Panella

Manager of Editorial Services:
Heather Talbot

Marketing Manager: Jordan Casey

Acquisitions Editor: Megan Belanger

Project/Copy Editor: Kezia Endsley

Technical Reviewer: Michelle Stern

PTR Editorial Services Coordinator:
Jen Blaney

Interior Layout: Jill Flores

Cover Designer: Mike Tanamachi

Indexer: Patti Schiendelman

Proofreader: Tonya Cupp

For product information and technology assistance, contact us at
Cengage Learning Customer & Sales Support, 1-800-354-9706

For permission to use material from this text or product,
submit all requests online at **cengage.com/permissions**

Further permissions questions can be emailed to
permissionrequest@cengage.com

Library of Congress Control Number: 2008929251

ISBN-13: 978-1-59863-558-4

ISBN-10: 1-59863-558-1

Course Technology
25 Thomson Place
Boston, MA 02210
USA

Cengage Learning is a leading provider of customized learning solutions with office locations around the globe, including Singapore, the United Kingdom, Australia, Mexico, Brazil, and Japan. Locate your local office at:
international.cengage.com/region.

Cengage Learning products are represented in Canada by
Nelson Education, Ltd.

For your lifelong learning solutions, visit **courseptr.com**.

Visit our corporate website at **cengage.com**.

Printed in the United States of America
1 2 3 4 5 6 7 12 11 10 09

To my companions:
Mimi, in whose kitchen I apprenticed
Brynna, who apprenticed in mine
Doug, whose kitchen I share

Acknowledgments

WRITING A BOOK IS AT ONCE a lonely and insular process and one in which the author is dependent upon and intertwined with others. This is particularly true of this project, which started as a simple book of recipes with photos and grew to take over my office, my computer, and my life.

As a project, this book is (as Doctor Who would say of the TARDIS—see http://en.wikipedia.org/wiki/TARDIS if you're curious) much larger on the inside. About 70 recipes made the book, while that many again were tested and not used, and the 400 images in the book pale in comparison to the 8,000 on my hard drive! Such a daunting task would have been hard to face without my companions, who have been every bit as clever, helpful, and delightful as The Doctor.

Doug, my constant companion, kept our reality together while I disappeared into my office for hours, or days, on end. He also acted as first reader for some chapters, first eater for some recipes, and my personal shopper on more days than I care to remember. I particularly appreciate that he never once laughed at me when I asked him to bring home dinner because I had been in the kitchen all day and only had three cakes and two kinds of cookies to show for it.

Brynna Owens, with whom I have cooked since she was a babe snuggled to my chest in a baby carrier, was invaluable, especially in the last weeks of this project. She spent a couple of days playing art director in my living room and gave the shelves of dishes that live in my office a serious workout in the process.

Where to start with the ever-helpful Farmgirl? From the earliest days of the wild idea, Susan has acted as a sounding board, offered moral support, sorted through potential recipes, covered for me at *A Year in Bread*, and talked me down from a ledge or two. She provided critical recipes and even pinch-hit on a single photo that saved me a half day's work. This book would not be the same without her.

If you are planning on being a semi-hysterical author, it helps to have a calm, cool, and collected agent. Fortunately for me, I do. Carole Jelen McClendon saved this project from oblivion early on with her expertise in managing contracts and crazy authors.

Megan Belanger at Cengage Learning displayed far more patience than I had any right to expect and never made good on any of her harassment threats, even as deadlines came and went. Kezia Endsley deftly shepherded this book through the development process and was invaluable to me as I moved my writing from the Internet (where there is always more room on the page) back to the confines of a book. I particularly appreciate Jill Flores, who laid out a half-done chapter so that I could see what I was writing. Patti Schiendelman listened to all my suggestions and did a painstaking job of indexing. I also want to thank the rest of the project team at Cengage Learning, many of whom labor tirelessly behind the scenes, including Tonya Cupp and Jordan Casey.

Michelle Stern was a fantastic technical editor, sharing her knowledge of teaching kids to cook to help me fine-tune the recipes and other information in the book. Michelle also contributed a great vegetarian main dish.

Ryan MacMichael helped me out with a marvelous collection of practical tips for what to do if your child decides to stop eating meat.

I'd also like to thank Brian Neely, who took time to wander the markets of Athens to take pictures for me. Tough job, Brian; sorry to make you suffer so.

Most of the gorgeous photographs on the chapter pages were created by Sarah Jackson, who shot endless pictures for me. I also owe a debt to her children, who spent days in the kitchen playing with food in the beautiful light.

Other people shared a recipe, a photo, or both—Katrina Hall, Kevin Weeks, Jessica and Sunrise Fletcher of The Inn at Lucky Mud, and Don and Kitty Speranza from The Inn at Crippen Creek Farm.

I particularly appreciate the following people who shared pictures of their delightful children having fun in the kitchen—Priscilla Armstrong, Bridget Axtell, Tamie Brown, Sarah Jackson, Jamie Prosser, Jessie Voigts, Jennifer Wickes, and Jon Yunker.

I owe more than they'll ever know to a small group of friends who banded together in the waning days of summer to brainstorm recipe titles and help me laugh in the face of looming deadlines—Emily Geballe, Helen Johnson, Alison MacLellan, Hosanna Lettvin, Linda Mayhugh, Anna Smith, Honora Wade and, of course, Farmgirl and Farmguy. You all rocked my world when it badly needed it, and I thank you.

About the Author

BETH SHERESH has been cooking as long as she can remember and writing about food for a number of years. Starting when she was standing tiptoe on a kitchen chair, she learned to cook from a series of masters of kitchen magic. As a pre-teen, she moved to a town without a decent bakery and taught herself to bake bread. Since then, she has taught herself many more skills and helped lots of young friends learn to cook, always creating a signature cookie for them along the way.

In addition to her primary website, kitchenMage (blog.kitchenMage.com), she writes at *A Year in Bread* (ayearinbread.com) and has a regular column, *The kitchenMage's Apprentice*, at Gather.com.

About the Contributors

MICHELLE STERN is the owner of What's Cooking, a certified green company that offers cooking classes for children in the San Francisco Bay Area. Michelle focuses on using locally grown, seasonal produce whenever possible and encourage families to spend quality time together in the kitchen (whatscooking.info/).

SARAH JACKSON is a photographer, mother, serial crafter, and zealous amateur cook. She lives in Phoenix with her husband and three children. You can read all about her adventures in photography, food, and craft at spjacksonphoto.typepad.com.

SUSAN THOMAS went from cultured California chick to manure mucking Missouri farmgirl in 1994 and has (almost) never looked back. An avid cook, bread baker, and organic heirloom gardener, she shares recipes, photos, and stories from her crazy country life on a 240-acre remote sheep farm at her award-winning blog, Farmgirl Fare (farmgirlfare.com).

BRYNNA OWENS learned very young that food was more than just something to eat; it was something to create with and to enjoy on every level. Under the guidance of her mother, with the experience of generations of women before them leading the way and keeping watch, she grew into a dedicated "foodist" and creative cook, while also exploring her other talents as a writer, photographer, and art director. She likes to share her knowledge and thoughts on her blog: playswellwithfood.wordpress.com.

RYAN MACMICHAEL is a freelance writer on a variety of vegetarian topics and is currently working on his first book. Read more of his writings on all things vegan at vegblog.org.

JESSIE VOIGTS is a mother, photographer, recent Ph.D., and publisher of WanderingEducators.com, an eclectic travel site. She loves to play in the kitchen with her daughter, Lillie.

KEVIN D. WEEKS is a former computer programmer who, upon finding himself unemployed, almost literally made lemonade from the lemons and became a chef. He has since gone on to grill succulent chicken in lemons and make the occasional batch of tangy lemon curd (seriouslygood.kdweeks.com).

THE INN AT LUCKY MUD is a magical bed and breakfast situated in the remote Willapa Hills of southwest Washington. They serve locally-grown food in a home designed for comfort, privacy, and gorgeous valley views. The grounds of the inn feature a regulation 18-hole disc golf course (luckymud.com).

THE INN AT CRIPPEN CREEK FARM is secluded on 14 acres in a quiet valley in southwest Washington. A small working farm is on-site, with chickens for breakfast eggs and pigs for their house-made sausage (crippencreek.com).

KATRINA HALL has cooked in a French bistro, taught Cub Scouts and middle schoolers how to cook, run a bakery business, and started an herb farm. She writes about her lifelong love of food at She's In The Kitchen (shesinthekitchen.blogspot.com).

BH NEELY is a black-and-white travel photographer currently living in Athens, Greece. Among his more interesting current projects are "Aphrodite's Hair," portraits of Greek women that focus on their thick, lustrous hair, and working occasionally as the photographer for the U.S. Embassy in Athens (bpsphoto.com).

JAIME PROSSER is a mom and web developer who loves to cook (and eat!) with her husband and two children.

Table of Contents

Introduction

I WAS ONE OF THE LUCKY ONES—born into a family that loved cooking, I have always come to the kitchen with anticipation of the pleasure to be had within. I learned to cook so early that, as with walking, I never thought there was any other option. This book is a celebration of that sort of childhood—one full of the everyday fun of good, healthful food, prepared by hand and shared with family and friends.

Children of many different ages can participate in cooking any recipe in this book. A four-year-old might help stir cookie dough and plop lumps of dough on a baking sheet while his ten year-old sister can make the same cookies more or less independently. Taking part in cooking also motivates children to learn various cooking methods and safety precautions so that they can do more of the cooking themselves when creating a favorite dish. All of the food in this book is made from scratch, giving children the thrill of creating a dish from the ground up, which is much more satisfying to a child than simply assembling prepared items.

This book is designed to involve children in all aspects of food preparation, from garden to grocery store to kitchen. In addition to the recipes, this book includes a Cook's Primer with a framework of information to start children off with an understanding of the big picture about food and cooking. Topics include nutrition, safety, basic techniques, interesting pantry items, and even a bit about how food is grown and brought to market. Some of these are complex concepts, but they are presented in ways that a child can understand.

Like many people, I love looking through cookbooks. Those glossy photographs are so tempting, but somehow what I make at home seldom looks quite so perfect. The secret, of course, is that food photography is an art unto itself; one that photographers, stylists, and others work for years to master. A crew of people work together on a single recipe—soap suds give coffee and beer that just-poured look; glue replaces milk in a cereal bowl; and colored mashed potatoes stand in for ice cream. Even the ice cubes are often fake! The photographs in this book, by comparison, are all of real food cooked in a home kitchen, by one person. This is real, accessible food; recipes you can reproduce at home.

One of the joys of cooking with your kids is the process of discovery that takes place as you search for unfamiliar ingredients, look for new recipes, and then head to the kitchen together to create something for the first time. As any good explorer knows, it helps to make a map of the territory as you explore, and cooking is no exception.

Forget what you may have been told about not writing in books. Cookbooks are organic tomes that are added to as you try out recipes and decide if they are a new favorite or need a bit of adjustment. You should scribble in the margins of this—and any other—cookbook, making personal notes such as what "medium heat" means on your stove, the perfect pan for a particular recipe, and variations that you try. The last of these is particularly important: when you create something wonderful, you want to be able to reproduce it later!

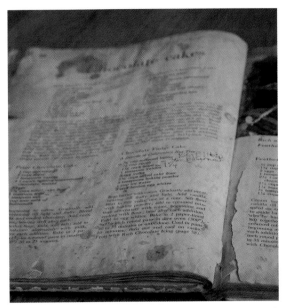

This is a much-loved cookbook, passed down through generations, open to everyone's favorite chocolate birthday cake.

About the Recipes

Each of the recipes in this book has information that can help you plan your time in the kitchen. Before starting a recipe, check the necessary tools as well as the active and total times so that you'll be sure you have the supplies you need and the adequate time.

> **Note**
>
> When calculating the time it takes to prepare a recipe, numbers were rounded up to simulate the effect of a toddler in the kitchen. It might not take you as long if your kids are older, or more cooperative.

Each of the recipes also has nutritional information accompanying it to help you manage your family's diet. There are a few things you should be aware of when reading this information:

▶ The Daily Values (DV) information used to calculate the percentage of required or limited nutrients is based on a 2,000-calorie diet, which is what you see on U.S. food labels.

▶ Milk is 2% low-fat unless otherwise specified. If you normally use non-fat, subtract 35 calories and 5 grams of fat (3 saturated) per cup in the recipe. If you use whole milk, add slightly fewer than that. In most cases, you can substitute soy or rice milk, if desired.

▶ Butter was used for nutritional information and recipe testing. If you use margarine, or one of the margarine blends, it should work well in these recipes. Some of the blends are designed for specific purposes, and some are unsuited for baking, so be sure to choose carefully.

I didn't choose these foods because of a belief that they are necessarily the best products for everyone, but because there had to be some sort of standard for the nutritional calculations. If you normally purchase a different type of milk, or margarine rather than butter, go ahead and use it.

Beyond the Book

I believe in the power of the Internet. Any information you could possibly desire is at your fingertips, which is an incredibly empowering thing for a cook. If you need a detailed explanation of an unfamiliar technique, the odds are someone has posted step-by-step photos showing how it is done. Spot an intriguing new fruit at the market but have no idea what to do with it? You can buy one, secure in the knowledge that you can find instructions on preparing it.

Some useful resources have been collected at this book's website: blog.cookingwithyourkids.net. There are also links to many of the studies referenced in this book, a store stocked with some great tools, extra kid-friendly recipes, and other goodies that just didn't fit within the pages of this book. (That's another nice thing about the Internet; unlike books, there is always more to read.)

You will also find the addresses of websites scattered throughout this book. Some of them belong to businesses, but more than a few are food blogs. You'll find websites where individuals who are passionate about food share recipes, stories, and some scrumptious-looking photos. Please visit these sites when you have some time to explore or are searching for a good recipe.

Picture Yourself in the Kitchen

Together

CREATING, ENVISIONING, PREPARING, cooking, and serving food is both a form of art and a participatory sport!

Kids of all ages enjoy playing with their food, and cooking is a special way to do that. It is also an arena where experimentation and creativity play a big role, and when you approach cooking as an exploration with tasty results, it leads to shared time that is rewarding and pleasurable.

There are additional benefits to working with your kids in the kitchen—it gives you more time each day to talk and share experiences with them, while cooperatively creating each day's delicious meals. This shared time every day provides the opportunity for teaching a wide range of general-purpose skills from "how to shop" to "how to plan a process" and "how to experiment, test, and revise your approach based upon results". The kitchen becomes a learning laboratory as well as a comfortable place for talking and sharing.

Parents: Picture Yourself in the Kitchen with Your Kids

PICTURE YOURSELF IN THE KITCHEN, with your child working next to you as you cooperate on creating a delicious and nutritious meal together. By participating in selecting and preparing the food they eat, kids will eat better and fuss less about their food, and will receive recognition for their culinary achievements. When you involve your kids in activities that are a central part of keeping your home and family together, you show respect for their capabilities and convey that they, too, are valued for their contributions to the family.

Unfortunately, there are no magical food fairies (although we all want them)—cooking doesn't just happen by itself, but rather requires our involvement. Preparing and cooking meals is something we all must do multiple times a day, and sure, it is always a bit of work (though it really can be enjoyable work). Helping your kids own this aspect of their lives, and giving them the skills to make it easier, will make an important aspect of their lives richer and more fulfilling.

When you start teaching your child a skill at a young age, it becomes a normal, easy thing to do. So don't wait. Entice your kids to start their culinary adventures while they are young and interested in *everything*. As you know, many a child has been eager to learn a skill at five and utterly disdainful of the same thing at 15. Even the youngest children can wash vegetables, smoosh things, or tear salad greens, whereas older children can handle more advanced tasks such as chopping the vegetables or baking the chicken.

Keep in mind that cooking with kids is fun—it is always an interesting exploration in culinary artistry! Sure, cooking is also work, but there are so many opportunities for play and enjoyment when you are sharing time with your kids creating today's meals.

It is certainly useful for kids to get into the kitchen with each parent individually, but to truly drive home the lesson that cooking is part of being a family, all of the adults need to get involved. If one parent does most of the cooking, make sure that the kids also get some kitchen and shopping time with the other parent as well—even busy parents with jobs outside the home can fit in time to make an occasional weekend meal. It is it important for children to see a range of role models, and besides, everyone brings their own preferences, sense of play, and specific expertise to the task.

Figure 1.1

Children enjoy cooking, even when they are very young.

Photo courtesy Jon Yunker

Figure 1.2
Children enjoy being part of preparing dinner for the family.

Photo courtesy Jessie Voigts

Among the reasons to work as a team on creating meals are the following:

▶ Work is easier and less burdensome when it is shared.

▶ It provides a shared set of learning experiences.

▶ Everyone will have more free time.

▶ With kids involved in making the meals, there will be less conflict over food issues.

▶ It provides repeated opportunities to create personal traditions and build family memories.

Working together in the kitchen can also help kids identify with their parents as real role models, in that cooking together invariably will show *parents are fallible.* Everyone has flops in the kitchen (it should be expected and accepted), and this will inevitably happen when you are cooking with your kids. The trick is to approach it as a puzzle and use it as a chance to learn both how to fix the dish and how to avoid the mistake in the future. This will help the kids deal with their own failures in the kitchen and provide them with the strategies to figure out what went wrong and how to do it better next time.

You and your family can eat much better food if you cook yourself—ingredients invariably cost a fraction of what commercially manufactured meals do. If you often buy meals at a restaurant, you may find that the cost of a single person's meal out will feed your entire family dinner. Consider the cost of buying pre-made salads at a grocery store (at $5–$7 per pound) versus the cost to buy the vegetables to make your own.

There are lessons learned in the kitchen that go far beyond the kitchen:

▶ **Math**—In the process of cooking, you use a wide variety of mathematical skills. From the basics of weights and measures, to fractions in both metric and standard values, cooks of all ages have to practice their math skills.

▶ **Experimentation**—Cooking is a wonderful form of organic chemistry, with edible results. Add a bit of this or that chemical and your cake rises, remove something else and it bakes hard as a rock. Learning the theory behind cooking allows you to improvise and create your own dishes.

▶ **Organizational skills**—Consider the skills developed in preparing meals. Kids learn planning (making sure that you have all the needed items), project management (arranging the preparation of ingredients), sequencing (which parts have to be done and in which order), timing (tracking timing of each dish so that all of the parts of the meal get done together), and coordination with others (working as a team with other family members to get all the parts of the meal completed).

▶ **Culinary and social dynamics**—Meal planning requires balancing a complex set of variables regarding nutrition, appearance, flavor, and preparation as well as the need to account for individual preferences and restrictions.

But If I Let My Let My Kids in the Kitchen...

LET'S BE HONEST. There are times when the reality of having kids means everything takes longer and there is a lot more fuss and mess along the way—and that's just the parents! There are, of course, issues with bringing your kids into the kitchen with you. Here are a few:

▶ **"...they will be messy (too)!"**—Cooking is messy. Flour goes everywhere, vegetable peels are dropped on the floor, and things are always boiling over. Don't look at it as having a child to make more messes, think of it as having another pair of hands to help clean. Show them the practice of cleaning up as you work—it is much easier!

▶ **"...they might break something!"**—Oh yes, not just *might* break something, *will* break something (didn't you?). So plan on it—make it something you don't care about much. Tuck your grandmother's china up on a high shelf for a little while, buy a few unbreakable mixing bowls, swing by a thrift shop for random cute plates and bowls and *relax.* Plan on teaching them the appropriate safety protocols for dealing with broken glass, and use it a learning exercise to show them the right way to clean it up.

▶ **"...they might cut themselves!"** —Knives, while an important part of cooking, are but a single piece of kitchen equipment. There are lots of things your kids can do without using a sharp knife. When kids are small, you may want to do the knife work and have them observe. As they get older, introduce cutting skills gradually. A butter knife will cut soft fruit like bananas or peaches and those plastic lettuce knives are surprisingly robust. Like all such tools, plan on gradually teaching your children the safe way to use increasingly sharper knives, so that as they grow they acquire the needed skills to safely work with knives and other dangerous tools in the kitchen.

Figure 1.3
Kids are not the only ones who make mistakes and a mess! This orange sauce was burned to a blackened mess in the very nice copper pan without the help of a child.

▶ **"...it will take forever!"**—Of course, when you cook with your children, it will take longer. Remember, you are not only cooking dinner, you are teaching your child basic survival skills, along with nutrition, organic chemistry, and some math. Sure, it will take a little longer each time, but you have to cook anyway, and by involving them in the process you are able to cumulatively teach them the skills that they will need throughout their entire lives. Preparing food is something that they will need to do multiple times every single day of their lives—they will benefit greatly by getting good at it early.

Kids: Picture Yourself in the Kitchen with Your Parents

It's fun. No, really! There are lots of advantages and cool things that you get to do and learn when you are cooking with your parents.

Not convinced yet? Okay then let's start with one word: Samples! Cooks have a responsibility to make food that tastes good and the only way to do this is to taste as you go. So sampling each of the dishes you are making is not "snacking," it is a solemn obligation (but you can have fun at it anyway). You can remind your parents that you are "just being responsible" as you taste the ingredients and dishes you are helping create.

Figure 1.4

After you drag your finger across the spoon to test your custard, you have to lick it and test the flavor.

The cooks choose what food to prepare, so if you cook you can help pick what you have for dinner. If you participate in the shopping and planning process it gives you even more influence over which meals you will be eating this week.

As part of cooking and creating meals, there are things you can learn and experiments that you can do (such as using different temperatures when letting dough rise). There is a little bit of science, some technical skills, and a bit of creativity all mixed together.

You can also impress your friends with the things that you learn. People who can't cook will think you are amazing because you can. Invite your friends for custom-made mini-pizzas as good as the pizzeria, with crust and sauce you made yourself. The possibilities are endless and your friends and family will appreciate your culinary treats.

On a purely practical level, you have to learn to cook sometime. Although it might be nice to grow up with your own personal chef who anticipates your every whim, you're not likely at that standard of living quite yet. Eventually you will have to cook for yourself, so you might as well make sure it tastes good.

An additional advantage to learning to cook and helping in the kitchen is that it demonstrates responsibility and shows your parents that you are learning new skills. As you gain skills, you will be able to do more things in the kitchen and select more of the meals and sides that your family eats.

Natashia and the Magical Chicken Soup

It was moving day—in fact, I had been helping 7-year-old Natashia and her family move for a few days now and we were all more than a little tired and hungry as the evening began. Natashia and I had been dropped off at her grandmother's house as her parents returned the moving truck, and she said that she was hungry and that she thought everyone else was as well. She was right, but as is common for people who are moving, a slim budget was stretched by the move and there wasn't extra money to just take everyone out to dinner.

"Why don't we make them dinner?" Natashia asked. "I bet they would like having food when they come home."

"Well, let's see what your Grandma has around." I said, opening the refrigerator. Her grandma had, unfortunately, been out of town for a bit recently, so there was very little in the refrigerator and the freezer—certainly, nothing that would instantly make a meal for six.

Natashia was disappointed, "There is nothing here to eat," she said, "and I really wanted to make them some food so that they could eat when they got back."

"How about soup?" I asked.

"But there *isn't* any soup," Natashia explained, "I already looked."

"We can always make soup," I said.

"You mean make the soup ourselves?" she asked incredulously. "How?"

"Magic," I said smilingly. Being a 7 year old and smarter than adults usually want to give them credit for, Natashia instantly disregarded my claim of magic and wanted to know everything about how you make soup.

"What kind of soup could we make?" she asked.

"Well, let see what kinds of ingredients your Grandma has...are there any vegetables?" I asked.

Natashia was enthused, and the treasure hunt for "ingredients" was on. Searching through her grandma's refrigerator, she exclaimed "Carrots! Onions! Celery!" and on and on, although some of the things she found ("Pickles! Chocolate syrup!") weren't exactly good soup making ingredients.

"We have some vegetables now, so let's see if there is some protein to go into the soup. Is there any sort of meat in the refrigerator? Or canned beans?" I asked, knowing there wasn't time for dried beans to cook.

"No, nothing," Natashia said, disappointed. "Wait! Let me check the freezer." Followed a moment later by an excited "Chicken!" as she returned, triumphantly brandishing a small package of chicken legs.

"That'll work," I said. "Now what about some carbohydrates—do you see any noodles, rice, or potatoes?"

After searching through the cupboards, Natashia announced her findings. "No noodles," she said. "No noodles or potatoes, but I found a bag of brown rice. Will that work?"

"Absolutely!" I said.

We put the chicken in a large pot of water to simmer. Natashia carefully added the rice, and we moved on to chopping the vegetables. We worked together, with me explaining and guiding Natashia as she cut the onions, celery, and carrots into bite-sized pieces with a sharp knife. After the soup had cooked for a while, I removed the chicken legs so Natashia could cut up the meat.

"We're done!" she said, as she carefully put the chicken pieces in the soup.

"Not quite," I said, "We still have to add seasonings."

"What seasonings do we need?" said Natashia

"Well, let's see what kind of seasonings we have…can you find any bay, basil, or thyme?" I asked. As she handed me spice jars, I explained. "We start by putting in some—a few bay leaves, a little bit of basil and thyme, and add a little salt and pepper. Then we let it cook for a few minutes, taste it, and add what we think it needs more of. But remember, we can't take anything out, so add a little at a time."

With a bit of tasting and experimenting, there was a big pot of tempting smelling chicken soup on the stove when the rest of the family returned.

"I MADE YOU CHICKEN SOUP FOR DINNER!" Natashia exploded as her parents walked in the door, beaming in obvious delight and pride in her accomplishment. "I used a sharp knife and everything!"

So we all sat down to dinner, Natashia beaming as everybody complimented her on the scrumptious soup.

Natashia was clearly overjoyed with the recognition she received.

Her mother, surprised that Natashia had made such a wonderful dinner asked, "How did you make this great soup?"

"Magic," said Natashia, grinning at me.

Natashia is now 24, and at a recent gathering talked about this, her first experience with magical soup, and how overjoyed she had been at the recognition of her initial success. Since then, she has continued her exploration of kitchen magic, with her soups in particular becoming a cherished addition to her family's cuisine. She credits this initial learning experience with giving her the encouragement to cook for herself, her family, and her friends throughout her life.

A Cook's
Primer

THE HISTORIC FOOD CULTURE in America has changed. People are busy, with more parents working full-time. Cooking skills have too often slid by the wayside. This combination makes it far too easy to succumb to the siren call of food that is quick! Fast! Instant!

Enough of that!

This chapter covers the basics of food and cooking. Opening with a quick look at what we have available to eat, I move on to explore tools and techniques. There is also a list of useful tips that will make your time in the kitchen easier and more fun. Later chapters cover a wide range of recipes for meals, sides, breads, and sweet treats.

What's To Eat?

FOR MOST OF HUMAN HISTORY, and apparently before we started writing it down, we managed to find a reasonable diet without any sort of outside assistance at all. People learned a few critical lessons—children were warned of deadly berries, for example—but, mostly, we followed our collective gut, so to speak. And we did pretty well.

Common sense served us rather well right up to the invention of processed food, and a little while beyond. But somewhere between the 1920s, when Clarence Birdseye marketed the first flash-frozen fish filet, and now, when it seems difficult to find fish that hasn't been farmed, battered, frozen, and shipped halfway around the globe, something happened. To oversimplify, many people lost touch with real food. The kind that has been referred to as "food your grandmother would recognize."

Figure 2.1

Healthful, whole foods should form the base of your diet.

Photo courtesy Sarah Jackson Photography

Most food in the supermarkets is produced by large companies using industrial feedlots and contains questionable hormones, pesticides, and chemical fertilizers. Their monoculture growing methods strip the land of nutrients. Depending on whose survey you believe, our food travels an average of 1,500 or more miles from farm to plate—less for processed, packaged food, and more for fresh produce.

The impact of this method of food production is most apparent with produce. As food production has centralized and the distance from farm to market to table has increased, desirable traits for produce have changed. Commercial growers of produce value uniform produce that travels well, so they can present essentially the same product to consumers nationwide. Vegetables and fruit that can be picked before they are ripe are also prized, and the ripening cycle is artificially manipulated during shipping and storage. The result of this is a limited range of cosmetically attractive products with merely a hint of the flavor that our grandparents enjoyed as a matter of course. The bottom line is that mass food producers chose the varieties that look best on the shelf, regardless of taste.

Sure, fresh tomatoes can be found in Wisconsin in January—bright red orbs tasting vaguely of tomato, picked before ripe and trucked in from Mexico. (Some people call this "zombie fruit" because it looks like real fruit but it has no soul.) Whether this is actually an improvement over a limited supply of sweet, luscious, juice-dripping-down-your-arm-ripe tomatoes is arguable. It is, however, unarguably profitable.

Figure 2.2
Shopping at your local farmers market gives you a chance to buy fresh food from your friends and neighbors.
Photo courtesy Inn at Crippen Creek Farm

► Food is fresher, frequently picked within a day or two of arriving at the store. Once you get that food home, it lasts longer since it didn't spend a week on a truck.

► You know the source of your food and can talk to the farmers about how it was produced. Whether you are interested in knowing what was used on your food as it was growing, are concerned about e-coli and salmonella, or are just in search of a new recipe, you can ask the source.

► You help to strengthen your local food network, which is ultimately good for the entire community.

► Your money stays in the local economy, where it can continue to enrich your community, which is better than shipping it off to a faceless corporation in another state or country.

There are alternatives to pre-packaged, over-processed food and flavorless produce, starting with what you are learning to do now: cook it yourself. Take a look at the organic section of your favorite supermarket to see what's available. Because the focus is on flavor instead of appearance, you may have to ignore a few unsightly bug nibbles, although they do prove that the vegetables are organic.

Growing numbers of people are making an effort to buy at least some of their food locally and there are many benefits gained by doing so:

Food that is grown in the area is not necessarily available in local grocery stores, most of which have supply chains that are not set up to handle small farms with small quantities of a wide variety of crops. Buying local produce frequently means a trip to the local farmers market, or even to the farm.

Figure 2.3
You would have to travel to Greece to get this assortment of olives, but you can bet that a farmers market closer to home will have equally enticing (locally grown) products.
Photo courtesy BH Neely

Small farms, growing a mix of products for the local or regional market, provide an enticing variety of color, aroma, and flavors. Local farmers markets offer locally grown produce, often picked that day, and frequently have varieties that aren't available in supermarkets. It also helps support small farmers, many of whom are having a hard time making it these days. A quick visit to your local farmers market will offer an alternative to the bland, industrial produce found in most grocery stores.

When you know how to prepare your own food, you are no longer at the mercy of someone else's idea of what you should eat. You can shop at your local farms and farmers markets, and find fresh local produce, eggs, meats, and poultry.

You can also provide some of your own food. Because flavor matters a lot, growing your own vegetables can't be beat. A ripe tomato, fresh off the vine, bursts on your tongue, vibrant, sweet, and summery; a flavor that justifies time spent tending the garden.

Figure 2.4
Chandler, says, "The fun part about growing tomatoes is watching them grow and turn from green to red. Then eating them is the BEST part!"
Photo courtesy Bridget Axtell

What's Wrong with Children's Diets

If the American diet has issues, what our children eat is often worse. At school, restaurants and, all too often, at home, many children's diets are seriously lacking. They are eating too much fat (particularly saturated fat), simple carbohydrates, added sugars, and sodium and not enough whole grains, fruits, and vegetables.

Quite a few kids aren't getting enough exercise. The reasons vary—overbooked schedules that leave little time for play, the lure of electronic devices, or schools that have eliminated recess. The impact of this is clear—the rate of childhood obesity has increased threefold in the last 40 years, bringing related health problems with it. Diabetes in children, for example, has doubled in just the last 10 years.

CAUTION

The Center for Science in the Public Interest studied the children's menus at 13 of the largest restaurant chains in the US, putting together a surprising 1,474 possible meals. Of these, 93% were found to have more than 430 calories, which is one third of the daily calories for a 4-8 year-old child—the age at which kids are most likely to eat from those menus. A huge 455 of the meals had too much saturated and trans fats while a whopping 86% had too much sodium. Some simple choices, like choosing water or low-fat milk instead of soda, and vegetables other than French fries, can help mitigate the heavy caloric load. However, parents have to be diligent about asking for and reading nutritional information at each restaurant.

Organic Food

IN AN IDEAL WORLD, organic food would be as widely available as conventionally produced products, and always comparably priced. Neither of these is the case right now, however, so most people have to make choices about which products are worth their premium price and which are less important.

Recent studies have compared the nutritional value of meat, milk, and eggs from grass-fed organic sources with conventional, non-organic products and found that the organic options offer a substantial nutritional advantage. They have found that organic vegetables may well have more nutrients than comparable produce grown using industrial methods. Theories as to why this is the case vary, but it seems that industrial food production depletes the nutrients in the soil, which in turn produces plants that are lower in some nutrients than their organic counterparts. Plants that have to use their natural defenses against pests also develop higher levels of micronutrients and phytochemicals. The specifics vary from crop to crop, and between studies, and it's a relatively new area for such research.

One recent study, for which organic and conventional crops were grown close together to minimize the skewing of results, showed that organic crops have more nutrients than conventional ones.

▶ Organic produce contained less lead, mercury, and aluminum than their conventional counterparts.

▶ Milk from grass-fed cows has up to 67% more vitamins and antioxidants, 60% more conjugated lineolic acids, more omega-3 and less omega-6 than conventional milk.

▶ Meat from grass-fed cows has less overall fat, more omega-3 fatty acids, and reduced risk of e-coli contamination.

▶ Eggs from pastured chickens have three times the omega-3 fatty acids, 40% more vitamin A, and twice as much vitamin E as the typical industrial egg. Interestingly, the kind of grass made a difference, too. Chickens fed clover and alfalfa laid eggs with almost 20% more omega-3 fat than a chicken fed only grass.

Figure 2.5
Milk from cows grazed on pasture has more nutrients than factory-farmed milk.

The United States Department of Agriculture (USDA) defines the terms used on food sold in the United States, although some imported food also carries other organic certification labels. Some states also have organic certification programs. Organic standards generally require that crops are grown without most conventional pesticides as well as fertilizers that contain synthetic ingredients or (disgustingly) sewage sludge. No genetically modified organisms (GMO) are allowed and food cannot be irradiated.

The USDA has four levels of certification for organic food, based on the quantity of organic ingredients:

▶ **100 percent organic**—100% of the ingredients must be certified organic. This is the label you will see on single ingredient foods like milk or fresh produce.

▶ **Organic**—Only 95% of the ingredients have to be organic. The remaining 5% need only be something not forbidden, like food grown with sewage sludge fertilizer.

▶ **Made with**—This label means that at least 70% of the ingredients are certified organic.

▶ **Organic ingredients**—Products that contain less than 70% organic ingredients can list them individually.

From the consumer side, organic certifications are great. You can glance at a label and be assured that the food you are buying is healthful and free of undesirable chemicals, such as pesticides. This may not be the only organic food in the store, however. Some food that is not labeled as organic is, in fact, grown using organic methods.

Figure 2.6
Some produce that is not labeled as organic is actually grown just like certified organic food.

Farmers have to work, and pay, to become certified organic. They must keep detailed plans and records of their farming practices, pay fees, and even operate as an organic farm for a number of years before the certification is considered. Many small farms adhere to personal standards that are at least as stringent as any government but don't bother with the expense and paperwork of certification. It really pays to go to your local farmers market and talk to the vendors about how they grow the food they sell. You may just find that you can get fresh local, organic produce for less money than you thought.

The Cost of Organic Food

Organic food is often thought to be much more expensive than its non-organic counterpart. Although this is true in some cases, it is not always the case, so be sure to actually check prices for various options in your local stores.

There are reasons why organic food, particularly from small farms, can cost more to produce; for example, one farmer I know hand picks baby slugs off her lettuce daily! That lettuce is picked, rinsed by hand in a small sink, bagged and delivered to the market less than 24 hours after it is plucked from the ground. It costs a bit more than the lettuce in the supermarket, but it lasts a lot longer in the refrigerator too. After all, the lettuce at the grocery store spent days being shipped across the country before it was delivered to the warehouse and finally to the store.

Coming to Terms

Natural—A minimally processed meat product with no artificial ingredient or added color.

Hormone-free—Poultry and pigs cannot be treated with hormones so only beef will claim to be hormone-free. Poultry and cows can be treated with antibiotics so food may be labeled as antibiotic-free.

Free-range or free-roaming—This requires only a nominal effort to provide poultry with access to an outdoor area. This is often a semantic distinction since chickens frequently ignore the open door and remain inside for their entire lives.

Pastured—Animals that are raised with unfettered access to pasture. There is also the implication of an all natural diet, although this is not necessarily the case.

Buying Organic Produce

If you can only afford to buy some organic food, you should rid your diet of foods that are more likely to be pesticide laden. The Environmental Working Group (EWG), a non-profit dedicated to protecting public health and the environment, publishes a list of the most contaminated vegetables and fruits, often called the "dirty dozen." A downloadable pocket guide with this list and other information about organic vegetables and fruits is available at foodnews.org.

Most Contaminated Fruits and Veggies

Conventionally grown versions of these vegetables and fruits have the highest pesticide load. The EWG estimates that people could reduce the amount of pesticides they ingest by 90% if they purchased organic versions of these items only:

- ► Peaches
- ► Apples
- ► Sweet bell peppers
- ► Celery
- ► Nectarines
- ► Strawberries
- ► Cherries
- ► Lettuce
- ► Grapes (imported)
- ► Pears
- ► Spinach
- ► Potatoes

Least Contaminated Fruits and Veggies

Along with the list of what not to buy, the EWG offers a list of conventionally grown produce with the lowest pesticide load:

- ► Onions
- ► Avocado
- ► Sweet corn (frozen)
- ► Pineapples
- ► Mango
- ► Sweet peas (frozen)
- ► Asparagus
- ► Kiwi
- ► Bananas
- ► Cabbage
- ► Broccoli
- ► Eggplant

Food for Thought

I T IS NOT SURPRISING that any serious discussion of nutrition, food safety, food policy, and the like would lead to controversial topics. Each of these issues has people solidly staked out on both sides of the argument, but probably more folks who are still confused as to what the fuss is all about. This section covers a few issues related to the American food supply that you might want to contemplate.

HFCS

High fructose corn syrup (HFCS) is a liquid sweetener derived from corn. The cost of HFCS is less than half that of sugar and it brings with it a number of other advantages. Because it is liquid, HFCS is easier to work with than sugar; it extends the shelf life of baked goods while keeping them soft and moist; it freezes at a lower temperature than sugar so frozen foods (like juice) thaw more quickly.

There are questions, however, about the impact of HFCS on the people who eat it. Some evidence points to a link between HFCS and various metabolic changes that may lead to diabetes.

Although the flavor of HFCS is supposed to match cane sugar, some people swear they can taste the difference. Because of this, there are small specialty markets for sugar-based versions of products, like Coca-Cola, that normally use HFCS. Coca-Cola made with cane sugar is available in Mexico but was near impossible to find in the US until recently. Now you can buy it by the case at stores like Costco.

Figure 2.7
Much of the corn we eat is first turned into high fructose corn syrup, an inexpensive and ubiquitous sugar replacement.

Genetically Modified Organisms

Some food crops have been had their genetic code altered in order to add a desirable trait to the plant. While the first genetically modified (GM) food was designed to provide additional nutritional benefits, much of the effort since then has been focused on making the plants resistant to a commercially available pesticide—usually one sold by the company selling the seeds. This allows farmers to spray their fields with large quantities of pesticides that would otherwise kill the food crop. The crops grown in those fields unavoidably absorb some herbicide, and while there is some argument about the effect of these chemicals on humans who eat those crops, at sufficient quantities some herbicides can increase the risk for cancers.

Other GM plants produce their own pesticides—skipping the spray and having the plant do its own killing. Again, questions have arisen after some studies seem to point to negative impacts on butterflies that nectared upon GM corn. Cross-pollination with non-GM crops is another serious issue—there is no way to control where the wind blows pollen, yet seed manufacturers often claim this accidental pollination as theft of a patented product. In addition, GM seeds usually have what is called "terminator" technology, meaning that the seeds are sterile, hence the plant is "terminated." A free-floating pollen that could destroy your livelihood is a scary prospect for a farmer growing organic crops with seeds they save from year-to-year, yet some farmers have faced just that dilemma. Not many yet, but it does point to some unintended consequences of GM technology.

This is no small question, either. More than half the soy grown worldwide is GM (almost all for pesticide resistance), as is 20% of the cotton and almost 10% of maize (corn). In total, the United Food Standards Agency estimates about 18% of the cultivated land in the world is planted with GM crops.

rBGH/rBST

Many of the dairy products available in the USA come from cows that have been treated with recombinant bovine somatotropin (rBST) or recombinant bovine growth hormone (rBGH), artificial hormones that make cows lactate more. Cows treated with rBGH and rBST produce 11-16% more milk (about a gallon a day) but, sadly, these hormones also seem to lead to a much higher incidence of health problems in the cows.

Some people also believe there are health consequences, ranging from early onset of puberty in girls to cancer, for humans who drink the milk from these cows or eat dairy products made from it.

According to the FDA, about 17% of dairy cows got an artificial growth hormone in 2007, although that number may be dropping. Consumer demand is causing stores—even large chains like Wal-Mart—to label, and, in some cases remove, products from cows treated with growth hormones. Monsanto, which makes Posilac, the commercial version of bovine growth hormone, recently announced that they are selling off that portion of their business.

Helping Your Kids Eat Better

KEEP IN MIND that you control what comes into your kitchen. If you have a range of appetizing and healthful foods on hand, but little in the way of high-fat, sugary, chemical-laden food, your children won't be eating much junk food. At least not at home.

While obvious, it is always worth a reminder that you are one of your child's most powerful role models when it comes to eating. When you reach for a snack, choose something that you would be happy to feed your child. If you tell them to eat a piece of fresh fruit for a snack while you are eating a candy bar, they are likely to ignore what are saying.

Figure 2.8
Make healthy choices and show your kids that snacks don't have to include packaged sweet and salty snacks.

Kids eat away from home a lot—roughly a third of a child's caloric intake takes place outside of the home, and frequently out of parental control. This means that you have to teach them to make wise food choices when you are not there to help them. Discuss their food choices and help them make good decisions on their own. Then relax. You can't control their every bite and you will only make both of you crazy trying. They will, of course, eat junk food occasionally, but don't we all? What matters is the big picture—how their diet looks over the course of a day or a week.

▶ Give children a chance to exercise some control over the family diet by making small choices, such as which vegetables to prepare for dinner or how to cook what you selected. Ask questions like, "We're having chicken, do you think we should bake it or cook it on the stove?" and "What herbs should we use?" Discuss your alternatives.

▶ Present children with a short list of acceptable options rather than an open-ended question. Ask "Would you rather have broccoli, green beans, or a salad?" rather than the open-ended, "Which vegetable should we make for dinner?"

▶ Decide which foods you are comfortable letting your kids choose and then give them as much free rein as possible. Save your battles for when it really matters.

▶ Water—plain, iced, or with a squeeze of lemon—is a much better drink than soda or even fruit juice. If you keep a pitcher of filtered water in the refrigerator, it will be nice and cold when the kids are thirsty. Look for a pitcher your child can handle alone, or a container with a spigot, which is both easy to use and fun for kids.

▶ Choose your indulgences wisely, but indulge. Lower-fat dairy products are generally preferable from a nutritional perspective, but if you really like good whipped cream, use it. Just don't do it too often. If you never have treats, you are more likely to feel deprived, no matter what else you eat.

Figure 2.9
An occasional indulgence is not necessarily a bad thing!

The Cafeteria Chronicles

School lunches are very different now from just a couple of decades ago. Gone are the days when those legendary lunch ladies showed up at dawn to prepare steaming trays of fresh-cooked food—there was, to be sure, mystery meat, but it was *freshly prepared* that morning! Now it's canned and frozen entrees. It's not a particularly appealing prospect for a hungry child.

There is hope though, and some changes are afoot. One notable type of initiative popping up all over the country is Farm-School partnerships, which help get food from local farms into public schools. This is probably the most promising avenue for real changes in your child's school lunch and something you can work towards in your school district.

The Edible Schoolyard (ESY), is a program that planted a one-acre garden and built a kitchen classroom in a Berkeley, California middle school as a means of engaging children with food. Started by Alice Waters and funded by the Chez Panisse Foundation, ESY recently spawned a sister site in New Orleans, funded by, among others, the Emeril Lagasse Foundation (edibleschool yard.org).

On the other end of the celebrity scale, Two Angry Moms is, according to their motto: A movie and a movement! Susan Rubin, a mother disgusted by the food in her children's schools and Amy Kalafa, a filmmaker and mom, made a documentary on the problems with school food, and some solutions. They are currently touring with their movie and encouraging school gardens and the use of local food (angrymoms.org).

What to Eat: Using Common Sense

A LL OTHER THINGS BEING EQUAL:

▶ **Eat whole foods whenever possible—**
The quickest way to tell if what you have
in your hand is a whole food is to look for
the ingredient label. If there isn't one, or
if it is primarily one ingredient, you have
a whole food.

▶ **In general, less processing is best—**
Nutrients are lost when food is cooked and
replacing major vitamins does not necessarily restore the food's nutritional value to the
preprocessed state. Even foods that must be
processed before sale, like flour, benefit
from being left "whole" as with whole wheat,
which is more nutritious than white.

▶ **Eat the rainbow—**One of the easiest bits of
nutritional advice for children to remember
is that eating a rainbow of fresh foods guar-
antees a range of vitamins and nutrients.
This is because different nutrients are associated with different hues of raw foods. Red
bell peppers, for example, have a hefty dose
of vitamin A, whereas green peppers have
very little. Darker and brighter food is usually
more nutritious than its paler cousin. Brown
rice is better than white rice, dark green lettuce is better than iceberg, and so on.

Figure 2.10
*An assortment of bright natural colors tends to indi-
cate nutritious food.*

▶ **Control your portions—**Learn what a serving of food is supposed to look like and pay
attention to your portion sizes. When you
eat out at restaurants that serve enormous
portions—and there are many that do—split
a meal with someone or bring half home for
lunch the next day.

▶ **Control your servings—**Serve the treats
from the kitchen and put the dishes of vegetables and salad on the table. That way,
when people reach for second helpings, it
will be healthy food.

▶ **Make appetizers part of your meal—**
Nibbling small amounts of a low-calorie
appetizers, such as vegetables and a naturally low-fat dip like hummus or black bean
salsa, while you are preparing dinner takes
the edge off your appetite, making it easier
to eat moderate portions at dinner. This is
also a great way to get more fresh vegetables into your family's diet since everyone
will be hungry and likely to eat some.

▶ **Slow down and enjoy your meal**—Meals should be a relaxed and enjoyable time for visiting with your family. It takes about 20 minutes after you are full for the message to get from your stomach to your brain.

▶ **Stop eating when you are full**—Don't keep eating just because there is still food in front of you—studies indicate you will eat a lot more food if you do. Similarly, children who are told to "clean their plates" learn to keep eating even after they are full.

Nutrition: Fuel For Your Body

FOOD IS THE FUEL for your body and you need many different kinds of foods to produce energy and maintain your health. The basic fuel your body uses is *glucose*, which is a type of sugar (a simple carbohydrate)—this is the type of sugar known as blood sugar. Simple sugars are more directly converted to energy, whereas complex sugars have to be broken down into simple sugars to be used to create energy. Other types of sugar include fructose (sugars found in fruits) and sucrose (a refined sugar, also called table sugar).

Starches (such as in flours, rice, and vegetables) are complex carbohydrates, essentially stored forms of simple carbohydrates. When you eat food, your body has to break down the food into simple sugars to provide energy and supplementary chemicals (especially amino acids, fatty acids, vitamins, and minerals) in order to provide the chemical building blocks for your body.

What Your Food Is Made Of

The main components of foods include carbohydrates (simple and complex), fats, protein, as well as vitamins and minerals. Foods containing substantial amounts of each of these include:

▶ **Carbohydrates**—Breads, pasta, cereals, potatoes, beans, peas, and many vegetables. Whole grain breads/flours are best, enriched breads/flours are not as good, and white breads/flours are least healthy. Likewise, natural vegetable starches are best while refined starches are less healthy. Although sugar is seldom called healthful, refined sugars (sucrose) are generally thought to be less healthy than natural forms like honey, and high fructose corn syrup (HFCS) is the worst of all sugars.

▶ **Protein**—Meats (chicken, turkey, beef, lamb, fish, and so on) and some vegetables (soy beans). Certain combinations of vegetables and grains (such as beans and rice) can also provide all of the essential amino acid components of protein.

▶ **Fats**—Dairy (milk, cheese, and butter) and oils (olive oil, canola oil, peanut oil, and so on), and meats, poultry, and fish all contain fat. Vegetable oils are healthier than animal fats, unsaturated fats are healthier than saturated fats, and trans-fats are worst. Certain fats (containing fatty acids) such as omega-3 and linoleic acid are essential in your diet. Fats also work in the intestine to promote the absorption of vitamins A, D, E, and K.

Why You Need to Eat a Balanced Diet

Our bodies are complex biological machines, requiring a complete complement of nutritional components including carbohydrates, fiber, fats, protein, as well as vitamins and minerals. The many different types of foods can be simplified into some basic food groups: the fruits, vegetables, grains, dairy, fats/oils, and meats. Although many of the food groups contain multiple of the nutritional components, a simplified view makes it easier to figure out how to get balanced nutrients in your meals:

▶ **Fruits** contain more simple carbohydrates (fructose), some complex carbohydrates (starch), and various vitamins and minerals (depending upon the specific fruit). They should account for about 15% of your daily calories.

▶ **Vegetables** contain some simple carbohydrates (fructose), more complex carbohydrates (starch), may contain some protein, and are a good source of many vitamins and minerals. About 20% of your calories should come from vegetables.

▶ **Grains**, which should make up about 40% of your caloric intake, contain complex carbohydrates and (in whole grains) fiber and are a good source of certain vitamins (such as B1).

▶ **Dairy** contains carbohydrates and fatty acids (fats) and may contain some protein. They are a good source of certain vitamins (A, B2, D) and minerals (calcium and folate). Only 10% of your calories should come from dairy products.

▶ **Fats and oils** contains fatty acids such as oleic and linoleic acids (needed fatty acids), but may also contain saturated fats and trans fats (which are less healthy). You should aim to keep your fat intake at about 5% of your diet.

▶ **Meats and beans** contain a significant amount of protein and complex fats (triglycerides) and may also contain certain vitamins and minerals (iron). Only about 10% of your calories should come from meat.

To get a balanced set of nutrients, you should eat foods from each of these groups, if not at every meal, then over the course of every day. The proportions should be roughly as indicated, yet the total amount of food one eats needs to reflect each person's age, size, and activity level. The USDA publishes standards for diets that are intended to help people determine what, and how much, to eat.

Figure 2.11
Beans are a good vegetable-based source of protein.

Table 2.1 Recommended Servings of Each Food Group, Based on Age

	Servings per Day		
Food Group	**Preschool**	**Elementary**	**Post-Elementary**
Vegetables	3	4	6
Grains	6	6	6
Fruit	3	3	4
Protein: Meat/beans	2	5	5-6
Dairy	2	3	3
Fat	Limit	Limit	Limit
Sugar	Limit	Limit	Limit
Total Calories per Day	1000-1400	1000-1800	1800-2400

Serving sizes are defined as:

▶ **Dairy**—1 cup milk or yogurt; 2 ounces cheese

▶ **Grain**—1/2 cup cooked grain such as pasta; 1 slice of bread; 1 ounce of boxed cereal

▶ **Vegetables**—1/2 cup of chopped/raw or 1 cup of leafy greens

▶ **Protein**—2-3 ounces of lean fish, poultry or other meat; 1/2 cup cooked dry beans; 1 egg or 2 tablespoons peanut butter is 1/2 serving

▶ **Fruit**—1 piece of fruit; 6 oz of juice; 1/2 cup canned; 1/4 cup dried

▶ **Fats and oils**—1 teaspoon oil; 1 strip of bacon; 5 large olives

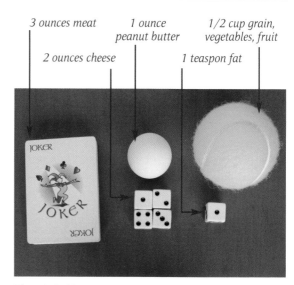

3 ounces meat   *1 ounce peanut butter*   *1/2 cup grain, vegetables, fruit*

2 ounces cheese   *1 teaspon fat*

Figure 2.12
Common objects illustrate the serving size of various foods.

The food from a meal is processed and the nutrients are metabolized during the four hours after each meal. To optimize the digestion and assimilation of the nutrients, it is helpful to have some foods from each of the food groups in every meal.

Calories in (Food), Calories Out (Physical Activity)

The "fuel value" of food is measured in calories:

- ▶ Carbohydrates (sugars, starch, and fiber) provide four calories per gram.

- ▶ Proteins are comprised of chemicals called amino acids and also provide four calories per gram.

- ▶ Fats and oils provide nine calories per gram.

Figure 2.13
Fat has more than twice as many calories per gram as carbohydrates and protein.

Calories are "burned" as you do activities, especially vigorous activities such as sports and exercise. Eating fat does not specifically make you gain weight, rather *all* excess calories are stored as fat in your body.

You can most easily manage this relationship between food calories in and energy calories out (due to physical activity) by controlling the portions of each food provided during a meal and upping your activity level.

> **NOTE**
>
> Visit mypyramid.gov/kids or a similar site for more detailed nutritional information for kids.

We all know that the vitamins and minerals in our food are needed to keep us healthy. Some vitamins are directly linked to maintaining health of specific parts of our body (for example, vitamin A is essential, contributing to vision, skin and internal linings, bone growth, and other). Other vitamins and minerals, however, are needed in the digestion and metabolism processes. Eating a range of foods that provide a balanced set of vitamins and minerals will help your whole body stay healthy. To help, the quantity of some of the most important nutrients are listed on the standard nutritional label you'll find on most food sold in the US.

> **NOTE**
>
> The nutritional information with the recipes in this book, as well as the labels on food and in most other places, is based on a 2,000 calorie a day diet. Keep this in mind when you are using this information to calculate your own nutritional needs.

Play with Your Food

Contrary to some popular sayings, playing with your food should be encouraged. Not at the dinner table, perhaps, but certainly in the kitchen.

Taste unfamiliar foods whenever you get the chance. In-store samples often include slices of fresh fruit, cubes of cheese, less common meat (like buffalo), and more. A careful selection of samples provides a casual way of introducing new flavors to your kids. Offer them a nibble of melon or a tiny cup of yogurt. Take a bite yourself. Don't just ask if they like it or not, talk about why. Is it the flavor, texture, presentation, or something else? Kids have rejected food in one form only to turn around and eat it in another; consider plain reheated frozen spinach compared to a spinach salad. Best of all, this is trauma-free. If they like it, great! If not, throw it away—after all, you didn't put any effort into it and it was only a small bite.

Figure 2.14
Tiny sample-sized bites of new food can be tempting without being intimidating.

Salad bars are another wonderful way to introduce kids to unfamiliar foods. Consider the typical restaurant salad bar. They typically offer half a dozen kinds of green and every possible thing you might have imagined putting on a salad—and some things you haven't—with an assortment of potato and pasta salads and fresh and pickled vegetables. Top that off with a mini-bar of what can only be considered dessert salads with fruit, marshmallows, and even whipped cream. You could eat for a week before repeating your selection.

As a parent, you can use this range of choices to your advantage, exploring new flavors with an adventurous little one, or looking for options with a kid who is mired in a picky eater phase. Hit the best salad bar in town for lunch and let your child choose from the offerings. A single small spoonful of each is plenty; this is meant to be a tasting menu. Talk about each of the things you try, swap bites, and have fun. The odds are that you will come away with some new favorites to try at home.

Dealing with Picky Eaters

MANY CHILDREN go through a stage of picky eating, frequently starting about the same time they start walking. Frustrating though it may be, there seems to be an evolutionary reason for this behavior. As children begin to walk, they are likely to wander away from their parents. In a natural environment, outside with early hunter-gatherer clans, a roaming child was likely to encounter unknown, potentially dangerous, fruits and vegetables. The aversion to unknown food at this age is thought to be protection against eating harmful foods, particularly during this developmental time period. Fortunately, most kids pass through this stage by about age 4 or 5.

If your kids are going through a picky phase, you might want to try a few strategies to get them to eat a broader range of foods:

▶ Try marketing good foods to your children in attractive ways. Many children who turn their noses up at shredded carrots will happily munch them down if they are called "salad sprinkles".

▶ Offer samples of new food, just like at the stores. Pick a couple of foods that you would like your kids to try and skewer bite-sized pieces on toothpicks.

▶ Try a bit of reverse psychology. Sometimes, a joking "it's too good for kids!" is all it takes to convince a child that those fresh vegetables are worth trying.

▶ Don't make a big deal of it. Everyone's taste in food changes over time, and foods that are anathema this week may well be favored next. This too shall pass.

Figure 2.15
Kids will eat a surprising range of foods if you give them a chance.
Photo courtesy Jessie Voigts

> **NOTE**
>
> Surprisingly, only eight foods account for the majority of food allergies: peanuts, nuts grown on trees, fish, shellfish, eggs, milk, soy, and wheat account for about 90% of food allergies. Although corn is not considered an allergen, there are increasing reports of people with varying degrees of allergies to corn. This may become more problematic because corn is an ingredient in so many foods and other products on store shelves.

Kids have all sorts of wild ideas about what combination of foods might taste good together and how to prepare them. Let your kids be creative and come up with their own dishes. You may want to try a bite of their invention before you reject anything, however, because that's what you expect of them. Besides, give it a chance, they might create something you end up incorporating into the regular family menu.

Weekends are a particularly good time to play with your food, maybe at lunchtime or for a mid-afternoon snack. It gives the kids a chance to try their own creations without using large amounts of food or requiring the commitment of a family dinner.

Playful does not mean complicated. You can play games with your menu without any elaborate preparation. You could make a meal with ingredients all starting with a particular letter—how about a pepperoni, pepper, parmesan, and provolone pizza? Every once in a while, blow off the nutritional advice to "eat a rainbow" and make a meal where everything is one color. Explore an ethnic cuisine by making one new dish at a time over the course of a month and then put on a final banquet, maybe even with costumes.

NOTE

Playing with your food can pay off in the long run, for reasons that might not be obvious until later. My 5-year-old daughter invented her signature omelet one Saturday—a hot dog (the blander the better) chopped up with Tillamook extra sharp cheddar and grape jelly. She insisted on making it for breakfast every weekend for years, offering one to anyone who visited. That spirit of experimentation has served her well over the years. Recently the same kid who created the truly dreadful omelet made up for it with a pumpkin pecan caramel cheesecake that is to die for!

Figure 2.16

If you encourage your children to experiment with food, they just might grow up to make you a scrumptious cheesecake from a recipe they invented.

Photo courtesy Brynna Owens

House Food Rules

EVERY FAMILY HAS RULES about food, either explicit or implicit. If you don't think you have any, or aren't sure what they are, ask your kids. They are likely to come up with some good ones.

A wise selection of house rules can help everyone eat healthier and will go a long way towards making meal times peaceful. Make sure that you have some positives mixed into your list. Here are a few rules you might want to use:

▶ Dinner must include a green vegetable or salad.

▶ Everyone has to take at least one "trial bite" of everything on the plate. These are also known by names such as the "no thank you bite." Tastes change, particularly in kids, so even if they hated something last month, it is worth another try.

▶ No soda with meals, and only one glass of milk. After that, it's water.

▶ You don't have to like what you are served, but you don't get to whine about it (and the corollary—you get to say "Yuck!" only once).

▶ There are "free foods." Things like carrots sticks and celery are designated as foods that the kids can eat whenever they want.

▶ If you "aren't hungry" for dinner, you can only have carrot sticks, celery, or an apple later when you complain about being "starving."

▶ The family eats together at least four days a week and no distractions are allowed. Reading, sending text messages, and listening to the iPod all wait until after family dinnertime.

For obvious reasons, these rules aren't just for the children. You really should follow them yourself as well—at least when the kids are watching.

Figure 2.17
The rules apply to everyone! If the kids can't have soda with dinner, neither can you.

NOTE

Many households also have some rules that are specifically designed to respect, and occasionally indulge, individual food choices:

▶ Each person gets to choose what is for dinner on his or her birthday. This may mean dinner out at a restaurant choice or a special home-cooked meal.

▶ Kids who help cook dinner get to make some decision about what they serve. It might be a choice between two vegetables one night and choice of the entrée the next, but some decision is delegated to the helper.

▶ Everyone is allowed a short list of food they just don't like and aren't expected to eat.

Oh No... My Kid's a Vegan! Now What?

By Ryan MacMichael, vegblog.org

If you develop a nervous tic at just the thought of your child announcing that they've given up meat, fish, eggs, and dairy, there's good news: you can survive. Both of you.

You might worry that your child's going to wither away to skin and bones because there's nothing you can make them to eat. Or that once you figure out what to make, you're going to be twice as busy at dinnertime. Or maybe you can't even conceive that someone could survive without animal products. Here are five simple tips to follow when your child tells you they're going vegan.

Don't panic. It's only a big deal if you make it one.

Even though you might not know a single other person that's vegan, rest assured that your child isn't the first. Estimates indicate there are between 1.5 and 4.5 million vegans in the United States. There's a lot of support out of there, especially in the age of the Internet.

Your child won't die of protein deficiency after two days.

As a matter of fact, many Americans eat more than twice the protein that their bodies need, which some research indicates can lead to calcium depletion, kidney stones, and some kinds of cancer. The truth is, as long as you're eating a varied diet with enough calories, it's pretty difficult to be protein deficient. Foods you might not expect (soy, whole wheat pastas and breads, nuts, and rice and beans) are great sources of protein.

In fact, nutrition on a vegan diet is easier than you might think if your child eats a varied selection of whole foods (admittedly, it will be hard to thrive on a diet of vegan chips and soda, but that's true of a poorly planned omnivorous diet, too). There are a few things you'll want to research like vitamin B12 and vegan sources of omega-3 fatty acids. Pick up a copy of *Becoming Vegan* by Vesanto Melina and Brenda Davis; it's the nutrition bible for veganism and an indispensable resource that should be on every vegan's shelf.

Encourage your child to shop and cook with you.

Get your newly vegan child involved. Your child should help plan menus, food shop, and even cook. It's good bonding time!

Figure 2.18
You can survive your child deciding not to eat meat.

Make family favorites veg-friendly.

Having a vegan in the family might seem to mean that you'll be pulling double-duty in the kitchen.

But consider whether anything you normally eat is already vegan (pasta with marinara sauce) or can be easily made so (marinara sauce instead of meat sauce, a cheese-less veggie pizza, or swapping out meats for some of the excellent meat analogs on the market).

Engage your child about why he or she is going veg.

A lot of parents are scared of veganism because they just don't understand why anyone would put themselves through something as crazy as a life without cheese. For those of us that feel strongly about animals' right to live for their own purposes, veganism is a choice to live one's life in an ethically consistent manner with that belief. Use this opportunity to talk with your children about why they've decided to go vegan. Read literature that describes that manner in which food animals are bred, raised, and slaughtered or watch videos like *Earthlings* or *Meet Your Meat* to get an even more vivid picture. You may be very surprised at what you learn and gain a newfound appreciation for your children's resolve to make a lifestyle change for something they believe in.

Defensive Shopping

WHEN IT COMES TO SHOPPING, there are two major schools of thought.

The first says to not take your children shopping with you. If they aren't with you, the theory goes, you will glide through the supermarket to the strains of classical Muzak, filling your cart with gorgeous, affordable, healthful ingredients, perhaps accepting a sample of delicious cheesecake (non-fat and almost calorie-free, of course), leaving the store with the contents of your shopping list and nothing else. Arriving home, your freshly washed children will emerge, smiling, from the house to help unload the groceries while proudly explaining that they cleaned the house and cooked dinner while you were out.

The rest of us—the ones who live in the real world, with actual children—laugh at that image. Grocery shopping is, for most of us, a chore to be sandwiched in on the way home from work and picking up the kids at daycare. This includes free cookies from the bakery serving as pacifier for kids who stretch from the cart to grab gaily decorated boxes of things they can't have; a quick race up and down aisles might be more about getting something, anything, for dinner over choosing a balanced diet. If you arrive at the checkout counter with its impulse purchase candy display before someone melts down, it is a good day.

Somewhere between these two images is sanity. How you get there is different for each family, but it starts with getting your kids involved with shopping. When they are small this may mean keeping up a constant stream of conversation about food you are buying. Your kids repeat everything you

say, so why not say, "too much sugar is bad for us" and "we don't eat trans-fats. Bleech!" Sooner or later they will move from adorably repeating it to asking what it means, and there's your opening to tell them. As the kids get older, you can teach them to read a nutrition label and send them down an aisle to gather known ingredients on their own.

One of the best things you can do for your child is instill a sense of skepticism about marketing, starting with telling them that just because they hear something on TV does not make it true. Tell them this repeatedly.

Figure 2.19
Teach your children to question marketing claims.

Teach your kids that it is what is on the side of the box, not the front, that counts. The health claims on the front labels, extolling the food's virtues (low-fat, high-fiber, and so on), gloss over the less marketable bits (large amounts of sodium, for example). Give your kids simple rules about the contents of food, such as no trans-fats or HFCS; no sugar in the first 4-5 ingredients; no ingredients they can't pronounce correctly (this eliminates a lot of chemical food additives but only works with young kids); and less than 10% of a day's sodium or fat.

When you go shopping, stick with the perimeter of the store as much as possible, where you will find the least processed foods. Fresh produce, meat and fish, baked goods, deli offerings, and even the bulk foods are generally distributed around the outside edges, leaving the center to be a no-person's land of processed and packaged products. By simply concentrating your shopping to the perimeter of the store, you can improve the quality of the food you bring home.

In 2006, a New England grocery chain decided to create a simple nutritional rating system for the food it sold. A team of nutrition scientists from major universities used nutrition guidelines from a range of public and private sources to develop the rating system, which assigns 0-3 stars to each item based on overall nutritional value. When they used this system to rate 27,000 products on sale in their store, they discovered that more than 75% of them got a zero rating!

Figure 2.20
Sugar by any other name is still sugar.

In an ideal world, government standards and associated labeling would help clarify the contents of various foodstuffs and make shopping easier. Living in a less than ideal world, however, means that you have to understand the meaning behind the label before you get to the store. Here are a couple of interesting facts about food labeling:

▶ The USDA allows a company to use the word "organic" in its name even if the food they sell is not organic. The only requirement is that "the company is not trying to mislead by using that name". Look for an organic certification or ingredients to be sure the food you are buying actually is organic.

▶ The claim of "whole-grain" on a food label actually means only that the product contains at least 51% whole grain by weight. Check the ingredients label to see the grains that are included and how much processing they have been subjected to.

NOTE

There is a lot of hidden sugar in food, showing up with names that don't have "sugar" anywhere in them. This is a list of ways that sugar might show up on a food label: brown sugar, corn syrup, demerara sugar, dextrose, fructose, galactose, glucose, high fructose corn syrup, honey, invert sugar, lactose, malt, maltodextrin, maltose, maple syrup, molasses, muscovado or barbados sugar, panocha, powdered or confectioner's sugar, rice syrup, sucrose, sugar (granulated), treacle, and turbinado.

This sort of thing does not make your task as a consumer any easier. Researching every claim on food labels, and exactly what it means, is an impossible task. Fortunately, there are some groups, and more interestingly, many individuals just like you—concerned, yet busy parents who want to feed their families a nutritious diet without going crazy in the process— who are doing the research for you and writing about what they find.

Visit www.cookingwithyourkids.net for a list of places where you can get current information about food labeling and related issues.

NOTE

Artificial colors are often used to mask the fact that the food isn't its natural color. Wild salmon gets it namesake color from eating tiny shellfish that contain carotenoids (the family of pigments that lend carrots their color). Farmed salmon, on the other hand, is fed a diet they could never eat in the wild—vegetables, grains, and ground fish—none of which have carotenoids necessary for the bright hue people expect to see in salmon. Instead, the fish are fed dye to create that particular shade of orange, selected from an industry standard set of colors, much like the chips you use to select a color of paint.

NOTE

Every piece of produce sold in a grocery store has a little sticker with a code called a product look up, or PLU, used when scanning at the cash register. Each variety of vegetable or fruit has its own four digit PLU, but some have a fifth digit. That digit is either "8," indicating a genetically engineered crop or "9" for organic. The PLU for a Fuji apple is 4131, while the organic version is 94131 and the GM code would be 84131, giving the few consumers who know the code with extra information to use when shopping.

Figure 2.21
The product look up uniquely identifies each type of produce at the grocery store.

Nutritional Labels

Reading the standard nutritional label is simple if you know what to look for. Remember that what matters is what you eat over the course of an entire day, not a single food item. If you eat one item that's high in fat, for example, balance that by eating lower-fat foods for the rest of the day.

▶ **Serving size**—It is easy to assume that a small package of chips or soda has a single serving, but you would be wrong a surprising amount of the time. A can of soda is a single serving, right? It is designed for you to drink directly from the can, you can't even reseal it and save it for later, so it's clearly a single serving can, right? Wrong! A serving of a drink is 8 ounces while the standard can is 12 ounces, a 50% increase in calories, sugar, and so on. And we know you are going to drink the whole thing. So you have to not only determine what a serving size is but what your serving size is.

▶ **Ingredients to limit**—Watch your intake of fat, particularly saturated and trans-fats, as well as cholesterol and sodium.

▶ **Ingredients to emphasize**—Eat plenty of fiber, protein, potassium, vitamins, calcium, and iron. Aim for at least 100% of your Daily Value (DV) of these items over the course of every day. You don't need to worry about getting too much of these dietary components from the foods you eat.

Figure 2.22

Understanding what to look for on a nutritional label makes shopping easier, and kids can help.

▶ **Percent of daily values (DV)**—In general, less than 5% is considered low and over 20% is considered high. Daily values are based on a 2,000-calorie-a-day diet, which is more than many people, especially kids, need. A slice of chocolate cake will, of course, be high in fat and sugar—it's cake, after all! That's no reason to avoid such treats entirely; just be reasonable about the frequency and portion size.

Stretching Your Food Budget

ONE REASON PEOPLE SAY they don't eat a better diet is the cost. Although it is true that fresh, nutritious food can be expensive, there are ways to mitigate the damage to your wallet while still feeding your family well. Consider some of these options:

▶ Go to your local farms, farmers markets and u-pick fields. There are surprisingly good deals to be had if you are willing to spend a little time investigating, or picking your own food. U-pick fields are a big hit with kids.

▶ Community Supported Agriculture (CSA) is essentially a subscription service for vegetables. A number of consumers purchase shares of a farmer's crops at the beginning of the growing season. The farmer uses that money to pay the expenses of purchasing seeds, planting and caring for the crops, and getting them to the customers. CSA subscribers get a regular, and ever-changing, supply of healthful vegetables delivered on a regular basis. One fun thing about CSA boxes is the element of surprise. You'll get vegetables that you might have never heard of, let alone cooked with, or interesting varieties of old favorites.

▶ Look around your neighborhood for people who are doing small scale farming and selling products from their house. There are surprising numbers of people who get a few chickens because they like fresh eggs and discover that, during the heavy laying season, at least, they have far too many eggs to eat. These eggs are often from pastured chickens raised in a very natural environment, the very eggs you want, and cost just a few dollars a dozen.

▶ Ethnic markets have ingredients you cannot find in regular grocery stores, often at surprisingly reasonable prices. They also may offer kitchen tools, tableware, and other useful food-related items. If your child is at all interested in food, an hour at a local ethnic grocer can be like a day at the amusement park, exploring a world of fascinating food they may seldom encounter otherwise. Talk to the proprietor about unfamiliar items—you may learn the perfect cooking technique or be given an old family recipe to use with that interesting new vegetable you bought.

▶ One of the best tools to help you save money while eating well is a freezer. Admittedly, it takes a little space and there is an upfront expense, but if you have the space and can afford it, it will pay for itself in fairly short order. A large freezer allows you to stock up on more expensive things like meat when it goes on sale, and produce in the summer when it is inexpensive and plentiful. Freeze your own convenience food to have on hand for school lunches or a fast after work dinner. Once you get into the habit, keeping your freezer stocked is a simple task. Every month or two, spend an afternoon cooking food for storage in the freezer, making items like soup, bread, cookies, and other basics like pizza dough and marinara sauce.

Cook's Tip: Freezing Food

Wrap individual servings of uncooked burgers and patties tightly in a double layer of plastic wrap and pop them in a freezer bag. Take as many as you need out of the bag and put them on a plate in the refrigerator in the morning. When you get home from work, they will be thawed and ready to cook. You can also cook them straight from the freezer, giving them a few extra minutes of cooking time and being very careful of splattering oil when you place the frozen patty in the pan.

Freeze fresh fruit in summer when it is abundant and inexpensive. Lay whole berries or sliced fruit on a plastic-lined baking sheet and freeze until solid. Carefully pick up the sides of the plastic holding the fruit and pour it into freezer bags. Use as needed.

You can freeze almost any kind of bread, wrapped tightly in plastic wrap and then placed in a freezer bag or other airtight container. Remove individual slices as needed, or thaw whole loaves completely at room temperature before unwrapping and refreshing briefly in a 350° oven. Dinner rolls and breadsticks are small enough to go directly from the freezer to a 350°F (175°C) oven for about 5 minutes to thaw and crisp them up before serving.

▶ Never make a single batch of anything if you can avoid it. It is very little additional work to double a recipe and freeze half. If you don't have adequate freezer space, you can still keep many cooked dishes in the refrigerator for several days so you can eat the same thing twice in a week. You simply have to buy some extra ingredients, but by cooking just once, you won't be spending any extra energy to cook and clean.

▶ Think in terms of multipurpose meals. Depending on the size of your family, a roast chicken may provide three meals. The first is dinner, followed by using the leftovers for lunch (like the "Crunchy Chicken Cranberry Pockets" recipe on page 94), and finally, use the bones for a rich chicken stock that forms the base of nutritious homemade soup.

Figure 2.23
A simple roast chicken can provide meat for several meals.

▶ Eat at home more often. Going out to eat is fun, but if you are stretching your food dollars two simple facts tell the story. Americans eat about a third of their calories away from home, and spend about half their food budget doing so, meaning there is a 50% premium on the cost compared to eating at home.

▶ Preserve something. Whether it is an old family recipe for jam or a new way to prepare your child's favorite vegetable, having homemade food in the pantry gives you a feeling of satisfaction and provides your family with food that carries more than nutritional value. Your great-aunt's cherry preserves bring memories and family history along with the sweet taste of summer fruit, and that is worth passing on to your kids.

▶ Planting a garden is the least expensive way to get more fresh vegetables into your diet. Growing some of your own vegetables means you can serve more, higher quality, produce for less money than if you bought those items at a store. As a bonus, kids who often turn their noses up at vegetables will try almost anything if they grew it themselves.

Grow Something!

IF YOU'VE NEVER HAD a just-picked tomato, you are missing out! The flavor makes the hard, pale things at most supermarkets seem downright blah by comparison. That taste is sweeter still if you add in the satisfaction of growing that tomato yourself. For children, growing their own food, even a tiny bit of it, offers a sense of accomplishment—and sometimes, *wonder*—at creating food from seed to plate.

Gardening also expands food choices because you can grow things that you otherwise might not be able to afford, or even find. Of the hundreds of types of tomatoes on the market somewhere, only a few varieties are likely to make it to a local store. If you want tiny orange tomatoes or purple potatoes, you have to grown them yourself. (And who can resist purple potatoes?)

When choosing plants, look for things you love and never get enough of due to expense or lack of availability. Good tomatoes (not the pale, mealy things at the grocery store, which are still not cheap) can be expensive. A good tomato plant costs a couple of dollars, about the cost of a good beefsteak tomato, but the plant will provide pounds of tomatoes over the course of the summer. Strawberries have a very short life once picked—one grower says he loses 99 of every 100 berries between the field and the consumer's kitchen, which represents a horrifying amount of lost and wasted food. Good food, too! Strawberries are a breeze to grow, however; so if you love them, buy a few plants next spring and put in a bed. You will be rewarded with berries for years to come.

Figure 2.24
4 1/2 year old Stephany, who grew this tomato her-self, says: "Tomatoes are yummy and red!"
Photo courtesy Bridget Axtell

A child's garden provides not only the joy of eating something luscious grown by hand, but lessons as well. To begin with, actually going through the process of planting, tending, and harvesting helps children develop their picture of where food comes from. Science lessons come from learning the proper balance of water, fertilizer, and nurturing. Gardens need care or they will wilt and die, which helps teach responsibility.

Planting a special small garden with your kids can start them on a life-long adventure of growing their own food. It does not require a large space, in fact, a container is the perfect place to start. Choose a few plants—some favorite vegetables, perhaps, or a group with a single theme or common use.

Front Yard Herb Gardens

Any small space can be transformed into a gorgeous herb garden that will rock your culinary world. Starting with the beds planted around the foundation of your house—the ones with blobs of "landscaping plants." Thoughtful plant selection and placement can result in a garden that will improve both your cooking and your yard.

The prominent location and shallow beds call for plants that are beautiful as well as aromatic and tasty. Tri-color and golden sage, variegated mint and thyme, and golden oregano all add multicolored foliage to the garden. Edible flowers add splashes of color. Mints thrive in the dry stripe under the roof overhang. Rosemary is a beautiful shrub, especially when it is covered with tiny blue orchid-like blossoms. Use creeping thyme to soften the hard line between concrete and garden. Put chive clumps in several places to provide spikes of green and intermittent flowers.

Figure 2.25
A close look at this garden bed reveals a mix of beautiful, and useful, herbs and flowers, including rosemary, chives, tri-color and green sage, and edible pansies.

Making a Kid-Friendly Kitchen

MAKE IT SAFE—small children need a boost to reach the counter so find a steady stool or chair that lets your small cooks work safely. Move sharp and dangerous devices onto a high shelf or other place that is out of easy reach.

Make it easy—consider parts of your kitchen that can be rearranged to make it easier for your kids to cook with you. Low cabinets and drawers can hold dishes and linens so the kids can easily reach what they need to set the table. Store a bowl and a jar of favorite cereal on a low shelf, and leave a small pitcher of milk in the refrigerator if your child can't manage the milk container, so your children can make their own breakfasts.

Make it fun—get a few special kitchen tools just for your kids. A special wooden spoon, bright silicone spatula, and an apron costs little but go a long way towards making a child feel at home in the kitchen.

Figure 2.26
Make sure your little chef has a secure place to stand while she works.
Photo courtesy Jamie Prosser

NOTE

Getting a few special utensils for the kids to use in the kitchen does not have to cost a lot of money, nor do the items even need to be new. You can find all sorts of kitchen goodies, even small appliances like waffle irons and ice cream makers, for a fraction of their usual price at thrift stores.

Age Appropriate Cooking

YOUNG CHILDREN CAN SIT at the counter and do homework, or just chat, while you do prep work that is not suitable for little hands. When you are ready for them, they can join you in the kitchen.

Even when they are too young to help with a particular job, talk to your children about what you are doing. If you say, "I curl my fingers back so I don't cut myself with the knife," your child will start to have an understanding of how and why to keep their fingers out of the way of sharp blades by the time they can use them.

If you start cooking with your children when they are small, kids who are in middle school can do just about any task in the kitchen. With literally hundreds, or thousands, of days in the kitchen under their belt, they will be mastering skills and gaining independence.

As kids get older and gain experience, let them do more challenging tasks in the kitchen. Let them do a little more each time and keep an eye on them, but let them expand their skills. Pay attention as you work together and when they are ready for the next bit of responsibility, let them try it.

Cooking Rules

Cooking is a lot of fun but there are things everyone needs to pay attention to in the kitchen. Most of these rules apply to everyone, but there are a couple at the end just for kids.

Figure 2.27
There are no set rules for when your child will be ready to take on a new task.
Photo courtesy Sarah Jackson Photography

▶ Before you start cooking, roll up your sleeves, tie back long hair, and put on an apron if you want to keep your clothes clean.

▶ Wash your hands with warm, soapy water before you start cooking and again after touching raw meat, fish, or poultry.

▶ Start with clean counters and cutting boards. Clean up as you go, taking advantage of those times between slicing and stirring. Put ingredients away, wipe off work surfaces, rinse dishes and/or put them in the dishwasher.

▶ When you are cooking on the stove, turn the handles of pans away from the front you don't accidently hit it and knock over the pan. Use a hot pad or mitt when holding onto hot pan handles or removing hot pans from the oven. Put hot pans on a heat-resistant surface, a mat, wooden board, or similar surface.

▶ Ask for help if you need it. This goes for both kids and parents.

▶ Kids, pay attention to your parent's instructions about safety concerns. Be sure to move out of the way quickly, if your parent asks you to do so for safety reasons.

▶ Kids should be extra careful when using knives and only do so when a parent says it is okay.

Figure 2.28
Lillie remembers to turn the handle of the pan so she can't knock against it accidentally.
Photo courtesy Jessie Voigts

Food Safety

THERE ARE SEVERAL SIGNIFICANT areas of food handling that impact the safety of your food. One major aspect of food safety is temperature. Bacteria can grow between 40-140°F so food should not remain in that range for an extended period of time.

- ▶ Refrigerated food with perishable ingredients, such as meat, eggs or dairy products, should be kept below 40°F. We all have times, such as during parties, when we need to keep perishable food out for longer than that. In that case, either nestle those bowls of dip in ice or put out small bowls and replenish from the refrigerated portion.

- ▶ Freeze raw meat that will be kept longer than 1-2 days. If meat is thawed, cook it before refreezing.

- ▶ Hot cooked food should be kept above 140°F and refrigerated as soon as it cools, after no more than two hours, or 1 hour on a very warm day.

- ▶ Keep uncooked food, such as meat or eggs, separate from food that is ready to eat.

- ▶ Avoid cross-contamination, which occurs when you mix two kinds of food that you didn't mean to. This happens when you are preparing food and don't wash your hands well between handling raw meat and other ingredients or if you dip a buttery knife in the jam jar. This is an important aspect of food safety, but it's also practical. Contaminated food is more likely to spoil and need to be discarded, which is wasteful and expensive.

- ▶ Wash vegetables and fruit before using, even if you are going to peel them. It might seem like washing produce that you are going to peel is a waste of time and water but if the outside of a melon, for example, is contaminated, the knife will carry bacteria from the outside inward when you cut it.

- ▶ The "use by" or "sell by" dates on food are handy markers to about when food is no longer good, but are only guidelines. A few hours at a slightly higher than expected temperature can take days off the life of a container of milk without a visible sign. Sniff food you suspect is bad, but do not taste food if you think it has spoiled.

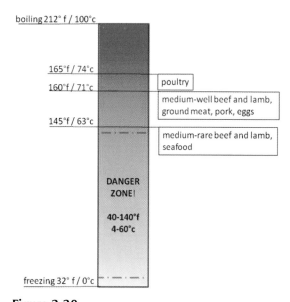

Figure 2.29
Observe the safe storage and cooking temperature ranges for food.

Kitchen Equipment

WHEN IT COMES TO outfitting a kitchen, you don't need much to start with. A small amount of well chosen equipment can last a long time without costing you a bundle. Shop at a restaurant supply store. You can often find products that are more functional and durable than those made for consumers and less expensive to boot.

If you can only buy one of something, make sure it is large enough for the biggest item you are likely to use it for. It is easier to cook food in a pan that is too large than one that is too small. The major exception to this rule is baking, where the size (and to some degree, shape) of the pan you use truly makes a difference.

Look for items that can multi-task. I use my one-quart microwave safe liquid measuring cup daily to melt and mix ingredients; transfer large quantities of anything from hot liquids to flour; temporary storage of food; and as a bowl for the kitchen scale, among other things. Oddly, the one purpose I seldom use it for is measuring since that is usually done with a scale.

Stove-top cookware that is also oven-safe is convenient, letting you start a dish on the stovetop, and put it the oven to cook without using another pan. Watch out for handles that melt at high temperatures, which are often the weak point in "oven-safe" saucepans and the like.

CAUTION

Teflon coating, the most popular type of non-stick cookware poses a health hazard to domestic birds, which can die from the effects of fumes given off when Teflon pans are heated on conventional stove-tops. If you have feathered friends in your home, you should avoid Teflon altogether. There are ongoing debates as to whether those same fumes are harmful to people, but Dupont, the manufacturer of Teflon, acknowledges a "polymer fume fever" effect of inhaling such chemicals.

Stainless steel or well-seasoned cast iron pans are excellent cooking surfaces and do not release hazardous fumes. Manufacturers (like Cuisinart) have environmentally friendly non-stick pans as well. If you do use non-stick cooking surfaces, be very careful not to heat empty pans over high heat, as it only takes a few minutes to reach unsafe temperatures.

Tools for Kids

If you have a dedicated cook who is going to be too young for knives for a while yet, look into other methods of slicing and dicing. People who aren't quite ready to wield a chef's knife can use scissors for a lot of things and even operate food processors (with supervision) or one of those chopping gizmos they sell on TV.

Kitchen shops have a multitude of gadgets that can be put to good use, not necessarily for the intended purpose. One of my favorite hand tools in the kitchen is this little dish scraper that costs about a dollar. It stands in for your fingers when mixing pastry, cuts and mashes soft fruit, and even scrapes the peel off of vegetables.

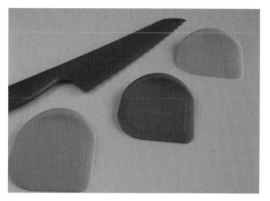

Figure 2.30
Bright nylon knives and little plastic dish scrapers are perfectly good for their intended purposes, but they are useful for much more.

Small Appliances for Small People

There are a number of small appliances that can be very useful for children who understand how to operate them safely. With the addition of these tools, kids can be more independent in preparing snacks and helping with meals. When you think your children are ready to use something, demonstrate how to use it, and then walk them through it a number of times. When they are ready to use it with supervision, correct their errors, but make sure you also praise them when they are successful. As always, use your own judgment about safety and your children's readiness to use any tool.

▶ Microwaves let kids heat, or even cook, food without using an oven or stovetop. Make sure your children are old enough to be careful with steam. Check out the recipe for "Magic Microwave Mac 'n Cheese" on page 110.

▶ Toaster ovens are more manageable than full-sized ovens or broilers.

▶ Blenders are easy to operate and the blade is tucked safely away. Kids can make their own smoothies for breakfast on their own from a fairly young age—as soon as they are old enough to make sure the top is on securely!

▶ Immersion blenders are a bit trickier than standard blenders, but useful for older kids. Remember to watch out for splashing hot liquids as you mix them.

Basic Techniques

COOKING IS LARGELY ABOUT the controlled transfer of heat from some heat source to your food. Improving your cooking can be as simple as learning to control the speed at which this heating takes place. Your stove has a range of temperatures; use all of them. Some people pick one heat setting and use it on all their food, all the time. Remember, undercooking is better than overcooking. Putting something like undercooked meat back on the heat for another minute or two is easy, but undoing that extra two minutes of cooking is impossible.

We use liquids that are heated to boiling, or nearly so, to cook food quickly and evenly. Several techniques use very hot or boiling liquid, usually water, to cook food. Other common cooking methods include:

- ▶ **Sauté**—Cooking food in a wide, flat pan, over fairly high heat. The idea is to quickly cook food, usually with a small amount of oil or other fat, without overcrowding the pan, which will slow cooking or, in some cases, release enough water from the food that it steams.

- ▶ **Fry**—Cooking in hot oil. Food that is deep-fried is submerged in hot oil, whereas pan-frying uses considerably less oil in a skillet.

- ▶ **Bake/Roast**—Roasting, which is usually done in an oven, cooks food by surrounding it with dry heat, just like baking. In fact, the real difference is the name—roasting is used for foods like meat and vegetables, whereas baking generally refers to bread, cookies, cakes, and the like.

- ▶ **Broil**—Cooking food with direct, dry heat, like from the heating element at the top of your oven. This is also how the barbecue works, but upside-down!

- ▶ **Brown**—This can be done a variety of ways (pan fry, bake, broil, and so on). Browning increases flavor in one of two ways, depending on the food—sugars caramelize or the *Maillard* reaction takes place.

NOTE

The *Maillard reaction* is a non-enzymatic reaction occurring between carbohydrates and proteins, usually when heated to about 310° F. This browns food and creates hundreds of flavor compounds that are responsible for many of the flavors we recognize and love. A few flavors rooted in the Maillard reaction are toasted grains, condensed milk, roasted meat and coffee.

Figure 2.31
Various sizes of cut food, ranging from bite-sized to minced, with matchsticks and julienne cuts in front.

When a recipe instructs you to cut food up into pieces, the terms that are used correspond to actual sizes.

- ▶ Bite-sized—About an inch
- ▶ Coarsely chopped—3/4 inch
- ▶ Chopped—1/2 inch
- ▶ Finely chopped—1/4 inch
- ▶ Diced—1/8 inch cubes
- ▶ Minced—Tiny bits
- ▶ Julienned—Long thin strips

Mixing batters and dough has its own terminology. Here is what it means when a recipe instructs you to:

- ▶ **Cream**—Beating multiple ingredients, such as butter and sugar, together until they are light, fluffy, and visibly increased in volume. Often used when making cookies or cake.
- ▶ **Fold**—Combining two ingredients by lifting and laying the mixture gently over itself. Folding maintains air in ingredients when mixed together and is used in recipes like soufflés.

- ▶ **Whisk**—Using a whisk to mix food incorporates lots of air for fluffy egg whites or whipped cream. Ingredients that need to be mixed well, but not beaten into stiff clouds, like eggs for an omelet, can be whisked for just a few seconds rather than several minutes.

- ▶ **Separate eggs**—Many recipes call for egg yolks or whites alone rather than as part of a whole egg. There are several ways to separate an egg and even tools to help. Probably the most common method is to carefully crack the shell in half and pass the egg back and forth between the shells, letting the whites drip into a bowl and keeping the yolk in the shell. If you use this method, make sure you wash the eggs well before cracking to remove any bacteria that may be present on the shell. An easier method, particularly for kids, is to hold a clean, cupped hand over a bowl and break an egg into your palm. Move your fingers apart just a little to let the white trickle through while keeping the yolk in your palm.

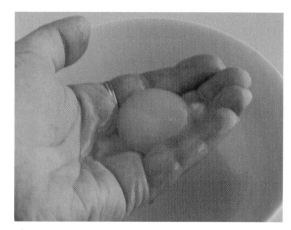

Figure 2.32
You can separate eggs using the palm of your hand.

▶ **Measure ingredients**—Dry and wet ingredients are measured in different ways, using different types of measuring cups. Dry ingredients are usually scooped into a measuring cup, which is then leveled off with a flat edge like a butter knife, or a clean finger. Measuring wet ingredients is done with a see-through cup that lets you see exactly how much is in it. Bakers, and a growing number of home cooks, use a kitchen scale for both wet and dry ingredients because it is more accurate than a measuring cup.

Figure 2.33
Most measuring spoons are for fractions of a teaspoon and a tablespoon, but there are also sets on the market for those folksy measurements: drop, smidge, pinch, dash, and tad.

Making a Meal

CREATING AN ENTIRE MEAL is more than just making two or three dishes and putting them on the table at the same time. When planning a menu, consider the overall balance of the meal and preparation process:

▶ **Is it nutritious?** Does it provide a reasonable amount of nutrients without too much fat, sodium, and sugar?

▶ **Are there interesting contrasts in the dishes?** Consider a dish like spicy chili with topped with cool, creamy sour cream and fresh, crisp scallions, or crunchy, lightly steamed vegetables paired with soft, but chewy, pasta.

▶ **Do the flavors complement each other?** Many combinations of food taste good together, even some unlikely ones like lamb, mint, and lavender. This is not universally true and you need to remember this when planning a meal. If one dish has very strong flavors, you may want to be conservative with the taste of other dishes.

▶ **What does it look like?** Does the meal look nice on the plate? If not, use colorful dishes and garnishes to brighten up an otherwise bland-looking meal.

▶ **Can you make it in the time you have available?** This is an important, if seldom considered, aspect of meal planning. How long it takes to make several dishes is not directly related to how long it takes to make them individually. On the one hand, there are potential time-savers, like the ability to clean and prep vegetables for multiple dishes at once, or using the oven to cook multiple entrees. There are also complicating factors, like multiple recipes that call for the oven at different temperatures.

NOTE

The Flavor Bible: The Essential Guide to Culinary Creativity, Based on the Wisdom of America's Most Imaginative Chefs is a great book that will help you learn how to combine food in meals, and can help you create original recipes. (To learn more about the book, go to http://tinyurl.com/4qpgnj.)

Although this might sound mind-boggling, it does not have to be. A simple meal of soup served with a crisp salad and crusty, chewy bread provides an appealing mix of flavors, textures colors, and even temperature. Foods from most food groups are present, and most combinations of soup, salad, and roll would pass muster nutritionally. Preparation requires one burner to heat the soup, access to the sink, and a counter to prepare the salad and maybe an oven to reheat the rolls—no conflicts for space or equipment.

A more elaborate version of this thought process goes into more formal meals, but the basics are the same. Once you get in the habit of thinking about these aspects of your meals, it becomes easy to create balanced meals on the fly without much effort.

Plan your time when preparing a meal. Getting the various dishes on the table at the same time and right temperature is no easy trick, especially at first. Make sure that you don't have too many things to do at the same time and look at things that can be done ahead of time. Before you start to cook, read the recipe all the way through. Make sure that you understand all of the terms and techniques being used. Check that you have all of the equipment you need and that it is clean. Verify that you have the necessary ingredients, or adequate substitutes, on hand. Make sure that you have enough time to complete the recipe, or that you can make it in stages.

The first step of cooking is one of the most important. The French call it *mise en place* (MEEZ ahn plahs)—literally, "setting in place"—and that is what you do. Clear your workspace, gather your tools, measure your ingredients, and do any necessary preparation washing and cutting vegetables, chopping nuts, and so on.

Figure 2.34
It is a good idea to measure, wash, and cut all of your ingredients before you start cooking.

In the Larder

A WELL STOCKED KITCHEN makes it easier to quickly put together meals and snacks without a trip to the store. The personal preferences of your family determine what you will want to stock on your shelves, but you may want to consider adding a few of these items.

White whole-wheat flour is lighter, in both color and texture, than traditional whole wheat flour, this flour is made from a white wheat rather than red. The resulting flour is better for making bread and other baked goods than regular whole wheat. You can substitute 1/3-1/2 white whole wheat for all-purpose flour in most recipes without changing the results too much.

Steel-cut oats are whole oats that have simply been hulled and cut into several pieces, giving them a richer, deeper flavor and chewier texture. Steel-cut oats take longer to cook than rolled (or instant) oats, but can be made at night for breakfast the next morning as in the recipe on page 66.

Oat flour is a whole-grain, gluten-free substitute for wheat flour. It is particularly good in crumbly things, like scones, or recipes that don't rely on gluten development: pancakes, muffins, and so on. If the recipe cautions against over-mixing, which toughens wheat flour, it's a good candidate for oat flour. Make oat flour by processing several cups of rolled oats in a food processor for about 60 seconds. (You can use a blender, but process about a cup at a time.) Store it like any other flour, in a tightly sealed container, for a few months. To use oat flour, replace 1/4-1/2 of the flour in a recipe with oat flour. If the recipe uses a lot of liquid, you may need to add a bit more as the oats will absorb more liquid than wheat flour.

Figure 2.35
Oat flour is a nutritious and flavorful replacement for wheat flour in baking.

Frozen juice concentrates are handy for instantly adding a concentrated hit of flavor to a dish. The flavor also stays fresh and bright because you don't have to cook off the excess water. A tablespoon of orange juice concentrate can transform a quick pan sauce for chicken into "Citrus Chicken Supreme" (or another cute name made up on the spot). Store an open container of juice concentrate in the freezer and only remove the small amount you need at a time. Look for concentrates that don't contain HFCS.

Stock base provides concentrated flavor (usually chicken or beef), that is particularly convenient for sauces, when you often need just a small spoonful. It is a thick paste that is stored in the refrigerator. Look for a low-sodium version.

Superfine sugar dissolves quickly even when it is not heated, making it perfect for sprinkling on berries or using in whipped cream. You can buy it in small boxes at the store, but it is much cheaper to make your own. Just put some sugar in a food processor or blender and process it for a minute or so, until it feels like fine sand. Store in a tightly sealed jar or use for scented sugar:

▶ **Vanilla sugar** enhances and adds a warm, spicy flavor along with sweetness, but without the added moisture or color of extract. To make it, put a few cups of sugar in a jar with 1 to 2 split vanilla beans. Close the jar tightly and tuck it in a cool, dark corner to infuse for a month or so before using. Add more sugar as needed. You can use vanilla beans leftover from baking, even if they have been split and scraped; just be sure they are dry before putting into the sugar.

▶ **Lavender sugar** is similar to vanilla sugar, only with lovely floral tones that add an ethereal note to fresh berries. Make it like vanilla sugar, but with a few spoons of culinary lavender buds instead of vanilla beans. Homegrown English lavender is perfect as long as it was grown without pesticides. Strain the buds out of the sugar with a small hand-held strainer when you use it and toss them back in the jar of sugar. Alternatively, measure out sugar with flower buds and grind in a food processor or blender before using—try it in buttery shortbread cookies.

Try This:
Spicy Cinnayum! Sugar

This is a more complex version of cinnamon sugar with nutmeg, allspice and brown sugar. Use it to make the fried bananas on page 86, to top pancakes or pastry or even just a quick sprinkles or even buttered toast.

Place 1/2 cup sugar, 1/2 cup brown sugar, 3 tablespoons cinnamon, 1 teaspoon nutmeg, and 1/2 tablespoon allspice in a jar with tightly fitting lid. Shake until thoroughly blended and again before using.

Cook's Tip

There are a few ingredients that are frequently called for in recipes, yet seldom on hand in most American kitchens. Fortunately, there are easy to make substitutes for the most common of these:

▶ **Buttermilk**—Mix 1 tablespoon of lemon juice or white vinegar plus enough milk to make one cup and let it sit for a few minutes to clabber. Alternatively, mix 2/3 cups yogurt plus 1/3 cup milk.

▶ **Cake flour**—Replace two tablespoons of each cup of all-purpose flour with cornstarch.

▶ **Self-rising flour**—Add 1 1/2 teaspoons baking powder and 1/2 teaspoon salt to every cup of flour.

A Collection of Tips

WHEN YOU LEARN TO COOK the old-fashioned way—at home from a relative or friend—you often benefit from their years of experience, distilled into a series of tips. Dispensed in a stream of no particular order, these bits of knowledge can be the basis of your own feelings of competence as you learn techniques that help you make your meals just a little bit better. Here, then, is a collection of tips that you might have heard if you hang around a kitchen a lot.

Photo courtesy Jessie Voigts

General

▶ Taste! A surprising number of people never taste the food they are making before it gets to a plate. Get in the habit of tasting everything, even when you know it is not yet ready to eat—bakers even taste raw bread dough to test it. Tasting food as you prepare helps you hone your cooking skills while ensuring that tonight's meal is pleasingly seasoned.

▶ Trust your instincts. This is easier said than done, particularly for the new cook, but it is important. Do you think that this apple bread pudding would taste amazing with pears instead? Try it! Have rosemary and thyme, but no basil for this bread recipe? It will still be wonderful.

▶ Adding salt to cooking water helps to break down starches in vegetables such as corn, potatoes, and beans. Salt added to eggs before cooking softens the protein bonds, making the eggs softer and fluffier.

▶ Preheat the oven adequately. Starting to cook food before the oven has reached the correct temperature changes the timing and can mess with the texture of some foods as they cook longer and more slowly than intended. This is true, to a lesser extent, when cooking on top of the stove as well.

▶ Use a timer to remind you of when to check your food. Don't count on remembering how long items should cook; it is easy to get busy and lose track of time.

Working with Vegetables

▶ Potatoes will brown better if you rinse them to remove some surface starch and then pat them dry with a paper towel.

▶ Substitute shallots in place of onions to add a slightly sweeter taste to sauces that use onions.

▶ Use bay leaves to add a great base to your soups and sauces.

▶ To keep peas bright green, cook them without a lid.

Figure 2.36
The peas on the left were cooked with a lid on the pan, the ones on the right without.

Baked Goods

▶ Soften hard baked goods by putting a slice of apple in the package and sealing it. Check after several hours and remove when you reach the desired softness.

▶ Any crisp-crusted bread that has been stored more than a day at room temperature can benefit from a couple of minutes in the oven. To refresh bread, place it in a brown paper bag, spritz the bag lightly with water (a spray bottle is handy for this and lots of other things in the kitchen), and heat the bread in a 350° oven for 5-10 minutes.

▶ When mixing batter, add ingredients slowly to prevent curdling.

Photo courtesy Sarah Jackson Photography

▶ When a recipe calls for greasing the pan, you can use the classic method of smearing a bit of butter or margarine in the pan, sprinkling in a little flour, and shaking it around to coat the pan. A spritz of non-stick cooking spray, butter, or margarine will also work. Moist cakes are likely to stick to the bottom of the pan, so cake pans are sometimes lined with a circle of parchment paper. To do this, grease the pan as usual, but do not use any flour. Cut a circle of parchment that just fits the bottom of the pan. Place the paper in the pan and press it down firmly so that it sticks to the butter.

▶ Parchment paper, which comes in rolls, is useful for lining cookie sheets. You can reuse a single sheet of parchment several times before it gets crispy enough that you have to throw it away. Parchment also makes for easy cleanup, so remember to use it for recipes that are likely to ooze sugar, fruit, or other sticky substances while baking. Plus, parchment paper is made from a renewable resource!

Working with Meat

▶ Slicing raw meat is easier when it is half frozen (but be careful, as the half-frozen meat can leave your fingertips numb).

▶ Slow cooking many meats, particularly inexpensive cuts, will make them significantly more flavorful and more tender.

▶ Searing meats at the beginning of cooking will help them retain their moisture, making them juicier and tastier.

Working with Blades and Other Sharp Tools

▶ When cutting food with a knife, curl your fingertips (on the hand holding the food) away from the blade.

▶ Always cut away from your hands and your body. If you slip, you won't accidentally cut yourself.

▶ Never put your hands into powered kitchen equipment, especially if it is plugged in.

▶ Sharpen your blades! Dull knives are more dangerous than sharp ones (dull blades cause you to put unnecessary pressure on the knife to cut the food, making mistakes more likely).

Presentation

FOOD MANUFACTURERS spend a lot of money trying to sell food to kids. They don't just throw that money around either; there is a lot of research going into figuring out what appeals to kids. Here is some of what they use when selling food to kids:

▶ Cute names

▶ Bright colors

▶ Fantasy and cartoon characters

▶ Samples

▶ Toys and prizes

You don't have to go to extremes or spend a lot of money to take advantage of all their research when you are cooking with your kids. A little bit of your own marketing can help make mealtimes entertaining and engaging for everyone. Try cutting vegetables into different shapes with cookie cutters before using them in soup or for dipping, or try a theme dinner, including food, décor, music, and maybe even costumes. You'll find more tips about presentation throughout this book.

Photo courtesy Jamie Prosser

Figure 2.37
An assortment of colorful tableware and linens can make even simple meals special and fun.

3

Off to a
Good Start

MORNINGS ARE HECTIC ENOUGH without adding in time to make a healthful breakfast for your family. Running out the door on an empty stomach, however, is a bad start to your day. What you need is breakfast you can make the night before, or something your kids can make themselves in just a minute.

This chapter includes quick school-day breakfasts like a luscious Berry Berry Smooth or the quick and hearty Sleepover Steel-cut Oats to make getting the kids off to school with a full tummy easy. Weekends, when there is a bit more time to prepare breakfast, is the time for an Apple Puffcake or Ricotta Pancakes with Strawberry Balsamic Compote.

Breakfast Matters

IT HAS LONG BEEN SAID that breakfast is the most important meal of the day, and for good reason. When you wake up, your body has literally been starving for 8-12 hours and your blood sugar is at its lowest. Your brain and body are starving, and you're still tired despite sleeping. For some people, it is hard just to get out of bed! Eating breakfast kicks your metabolism into higher gear and gives you fuel to get started for the day.

Depending on which study you read, however, any-where from a quarter to a third of us skip breakfast at least a few times a week. This means that a lot of people are starting their days at a serious energy deficit. This leads to grabbing whatever is handy, which is all too often sweet or fat-laden snack foods—not a very good way to fuel an active body.

One of the most apparent benefits of a healthful breakfast is mental. People who eat breakfast show improved concentration and productivity, whereas kids who regularly eat breakfast do better in school. The American Diabetes Association found that kids who ate breakfast were more likely to be alert, and had improved problem-solving skills, concentration, and eye-hand coordination—all important for doing well in school.

There also seem to be positive effects on the over-all diet of breakfast-eaters, seemingly regardless of the actual nutritional content of breakfast. Studies have shown that people who eat breakfast have a diet that is lower in fat and cholesterol and higher in overall vitamins and minerals.

Figure 3.1
Starting the day with a good breakfast is one way to help your child do well in school.
Photo courtesy Tamie Brown

Eating breakfast also seems to correspond with better weight management. Although the rela-tionship between breakfast and weight control is not exactly clear, with obesity on the rise in the US, it makes sense to give your family whatever advantages are within reach.

About that Sugary Breakfast Cereal...

A walk down the cereal aisle in a grocery store must be odd for anyone who did not grow up in this culture. More than a few of the offerings for the "most important meal of the day" are a weird mix of cartoon characters and cleverly disguised sugar—marshmallows, fruit bits, and an awful lot of boxes with some form of "chocolate" screaming on the front of the box.

If you were buying snacks, some of these cereals might not be too bad of a choice, but as a way to start the day, it seems to be asking for a short burst of energy followed by a mid-morning crash when all that sugar burns off.

Many kids, however, are really attached to their favorite breakfast cereal and won't give it up without a fight. Rather than remove the cereal from the house entirely, at least at first, serve it as a treat rather than a meal. Even if it is not *your* favored dessert, some children would happily trade a cookie for their beloved CrazyChocoCartoon cereal, and a small bag of dry cereal makes for easy munching on the run. That way, your child won't miss his cartoon- and chocolate-filled cereal entirely.

Look for breakfast options that provide about 25% of your caloric intake for the day. Many nutritionists recommend choosing one item from at least three of these groups:

▶ **Grains**—Whole grain baked goods, cereal, or crackers

▶ **Vegetables and fruit**—Whole vegetables, fruit, or juice without added sugar

▶ **Dairy**—Low-fat or non-fat milk, yogurt, or cheese

▶ **Protein**—An egg, nut butter, lean meat, poultry, or fish

It's All in the Growing....

Don't be afraid to serve your family eggs. Although they sometimes get a bad rap due to their cholesterol content, many dieticians (and the American Heart Association) believe that an egg a day can be part of a healthy diet. There is, however, evidence to suggest that eating a whole egg is better for you than eating the yolk alone.

If you would like to give your family the best eggs possible, look for eggs from pastured hens. A study by Mother Earth News found that, compared to conventionally produced eggs, pastured hen eggs have:

▶ A forth less saturated fat

▶ A third less cholesterol

▶ Twice the omega-3 fatty acids

▶ Three times the vitamin E

▶ Seven times the beta-carotene

▶ 60% more vitamin A

Figure 3.2
Studies have shown that the eggs from chickens that hunt and peck for their food in a pasture are better for you than the typical eggs at the grocery store.

Ricotta Pancakes with Strawberry Balsamic Compote

H IGH PROTEIN PANCAKES pair with a quick strawberry topping in this recipe for a light, yet filling, breakfast. Because these pancakes don't rely on flour for most of their structure, you can easily make a gluten-free version, by substituting oat flour or your favorite alternative flour. An original creation of Brynna of Plays Well With Food (PlaysWellWithFood.wordpress.com)—who happens to be my daughter—this recipe shows that if you let children play with their food, they will probably continue to do so as an adult...with delicious results!

Serves 3 (about 9 pancakes)

Active Time: 20 minutes

Total Time: 20 minutes

Tools: Small saucepan, wooden spoon, mixing bowl, whisk, spatula, and griddle or large, flat frying pan

Nutritional Information per Serving: 323 Calories; 11g Fat (30.9% calories from fat); 18g Protein; 39g Carbohydrate; 5g Dietary Fiber; 170mg Cholesterol; 334mg Sodium

Ingredients

1 pint strawberries

1 tablespoon balsamic vinegar

1 teaspoon sugar

1 cup part-skim ricotta cheese

1/2 cup low-fat milk

2 large eggs

1/2 tablespoon fresh lemon juice

Zest of 1 lemon

1/2 cup whole wheat flour

1 teaspoon baking powder

2 tablespoon sugar

1/4 teaspoon nutmeg

1/4 teaspoon cinnamon

Directions

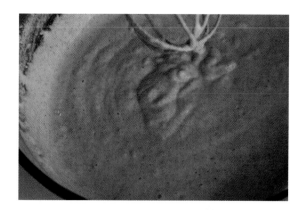

1. Slice strawberries into a small saucepan. Stir in the sugar and balsamic vinegar and cook over low heat, stirring occasionally, while you prepare the pancakes. Remove from heat after 5-10 minutes, once the berries soften and the sauce thickens a bit—this process will take longer with frozen berries.

3. Mix flour, baking powder, sugar, cinnamon, and nutmeg together. Slowly whisk dry ingredients into wet ingredients until incorporated.

2. Mix ricotta, milk, eggs, and lemon juice and zest together in a mixing bowl until well combined.

4. Spray your pan/griddle with non-stick spray (or use butter). Pour 1/4 cup of batter onto pan for each pancake. Cook until golden brown; flip over only once. Top with warm strawberry compote.

Eggs Ahoy!

AHOY, MATIES! The perfect breakfast for Talk Like a Pirate Day (September 19th), this dish combines eggs and toast in a single pan. Serve with a glass of 100% fruit juice for a home-cooked breakfast in a flash. You can use different shaped cookie cutters, as long as the center is large enough to hold the egg yolk.

Serves 1

Active Time: 5 minutes

Total Time: 10 minutes

Tools: Cookie cutter, skillet, and spatula

Nutritional Information per Serving: 194 Calories; 9g Fat (39.2% calories from fat); 10g Protein; 20g Carbohydrate; 3g Dietary Fiber; 217mg Cholesterol; 311mg Sodium

Ingredients

1 slice whole grain bread

1/2 teaspoon butter

1 egg

Directions

1. Lightly butter both sides of the bread. Cut out the center of the slice of bread with a round cookie cutter.

2. Heat a skillet over medium-low heat for a few minutes to preheat. Place both pieces of bread in the skillet. Break the egg into the cutout center of the bread slice.

3. Cook until egg starts to set, and then flip and cook for another minute.

4. To serve, place bread with egg on a plate. Partially cover the egg with the circle of bread, like a pirate's eye patch. (If you are also serving bacon, use it for the "string" that holds on the eye patch.) Serve immediately.

NOTE

These eggs have many different names—egg in a frame, toad in a hole, chicken in a basket, egg on a raft, and bull's eye—among others. Pirate's eyes, however, are the only ones that give you an excuse to say *Arrrr!* at the breakfast table!

Sleepover Steel-Cut Oats

S TEEL-CUT OATS, also known as Scotch or Pinhead Oats, have a nuttier, more robust flavor than rolled oats but take longer to cook. These oats are mostly cooked at night before you go to bed, leaving only a quick heating in the morning to finish.

Serves 4

Active Time: 5 minutes

Total Time: Overnight

Tools: Saucepan and wooden spoon

Nutritional Information per Serving: 223 Calories; 3g Fat (13% calories from fat); 6g Protein; 39g Carbohydrate; 6g Dietary Fiber; 0mg Cholesterol; 74mg Sodium

Ingredients

4 cups water

1 cup steel-cut oats

1 pinch salt

1/2 teaspoon ground cinnamon

Directions

1. In the evening, bring water to a boil in a saucepan. Stir in oats, cinnamon, and salt. Cook over medium heat, stirring occasionally, for 10 minutes. Remove from heat, cover, and leave on the back of stove until morning.

2. In the morning, heat oats in a saucepan over medium-low heat for a few minutes, stirring occasionally, until the oats are hot. Alternatively, you can heat a bowl of oats in the microwave on high for 1-3 minutes, stirring once or twice.

Cook's Tip

Let the kids choose different fresh or dried fruit and other toppings to keep it interesting. Try one of these ideas:

▶ Grate an apple into the oats in the morning before heating it.

▶ Cut up a few dried apricots with scissors, add some chopped almonds, and drizzle some maple syrup.

▶ Slice a fresh banana into the oats, add some raisins, and sweeten it with a little honey.

Cook's Tip

These oats will keep in the refrigerator for about five days, so you can make up a big batch on Sunday night and heat just enough for breakfast each morning. After cooking in step 1, cover the pot and let the oats cool to room temperature. Scoop any oats that you aren't eating for breakfast tomorrow into a container, cover tightly, and refrigerate. You can also freeze cooked oats, in individual servings, for several months. In the morning, reheat enough oats for breakfast, leaving the rest for later in the week.

Berry Berry Smooth

S WEET SUMMER BERRIES, tart yogurt, and a hint of maple syrup give this fruit smoothie a rich flavor. Low in fat, high in fiber and protein, with a generous helping of vitamin C, calcium, and riboflavin, yet tasting surprisingly like a fruity milkshake, this is a breakfast any kid could love. Use any fresh or frozen fruit you like in place of the berries for endless variations.

Serves 1

Active Time: 5 minutes

Total Time: 5 minutes

Tools: Blender

Nutritional Information per Serving: 243 Calories; 8g Fat (28.1% calories from fat); 8g Protein; 38g Carbohydrate; 8g Dietary Fiber; 16mg Cholesterol; 71mg Sodium

Ingredients

2/3 cup blueberries

1/3 cup raspberries

1/2 cup yogurt

1 teaspoon maple syrup

1/4 cup orange juice

1 tablespoon flax seed, ground

1/2 cup ice cubes (3-4 average sized cubes)

Directions

1. Place all ingredients in a blender and process on high for 30-45 seconds, until it's thick like a milkshake. You can usually hear the change in the sound of the blender when there are no more large chunks of ice. Serve immediately.

Cook's Tip

Some kids really like smoothies and will create their own variation most mornings. Encourage experimentation with fresh and frozen fruit, different sweeteners, and other tasty add-ins—like the chocolate chips in the next recipe.

Try This:
Overnight Smoothies

Place the juice in the blender, followed by the fruit, maple syrup, and yogurt. Cover and refrigerate overnight. In the morning, add the ground flax seed and ice cubes and blend for a tasty and nutritious breakfast in about a minute.

TIP

Smoothies taste great but after a while they can look sort of boring. Since the only thing you have to work with for presentation is the glass, why not make it really special? Go to a thrift shop and let your child pick a personal smoothie glass. They might choose a heavy glass goblet, a funky old pewter beer mug, or an outrageously bright plastic cup; the main requirement is that it makes them happy when they use it for a quick and nutritious breakfast.

Nutty 'Nanner Chip Smoothie

THREE PERENNIAL KID FAVORITES—nuts, bananas, and chocolate—come together in this luscious breakfast drink. This smoothie may taste like dessert, but it is high in protein, fiber, potassium, calcium, and riboflavin as well as vitamins C and B6.

Serves 1

Active Time: 5 minutes

Total Time: 5 minutes

Tools: Blender or immersion blender

Nutritional Information per Serving: 338 Calories; 13g Fat (32% calories from fat); 13g Protein; 48g Carbohydrate; 6g Dietary Fiber; 7mg Cholesterol; 123mg Sodium

Ingredients

1/2 cup non-fat yogurt

1/4 cup low-fat milk

1 tablespoon almond butter

1 banana

1 teaspoon chocolate chips

1 tablespoon flax seed, ground

Directions

1. Place all ingredients in a blender and puree on high for a few seconds until it is mostly smooth with lots of chocolate flecks. Serve immediately.

Cook's Tip

If you have an immersion blender, you can blend smoothies that do not use ice, like this one, right in the glass, as long as it is the right kind of glass. Pick one that is wide enough so that the blender can fit all the way to the bottom and heavy enough not to chip—use sturdy glass, heavy plastic, or even metal.

Try This:
Smoothie Variations

The nut butter and chocolate chips give this smoothie a lot of its flavor, so varying those ingredients can change the taste of this smoothie quite a bit without significantly changing the nutritional profile. Try some of these combinations.

▶ Double the nut flavor by using peanut butter instead of almond and peanut butter chips instead of chocolate.

▶ Macadamia butter and butterscotch is a warm, caramel-tasting combination.

▶ Smooth out the texture by using one tablespoon of hazelnut chocolate spread (such as Nutella) in place of the almond butter and chocolate chips.

Apple Puffcake

W HO CAN RESIST this eggy puff topped with fragrant apple slices sautéed in butter and cinnamon? Despite its impressive appearance, it is as simple to mix as pancakes and, with the right pan, puffs up reliably. Like a soufflé, the puffcake starts to deflate as soon as it leaves the oven, so gather the family at the table before you take it out of the oven.

Serves 4

Active Time: 10 minutes

Total Time: 45 minutes

Tools: Mixing bowl, whisk, 11" cast iron skillet (see note), hot pad, knife, small skillet, and spatula

Nutritional Information per Serving: 281 Calories; 17g Fat (52.5% calories from fat); 8g Protein; 26g Carbohydrate; 3g Dietary Fiber; 194mg Cholesterol; 185mg Sodium

Ingredients

Puffcake

3 eggs

1/2 cup low-fat milk

1/2 cup all-purpose flour

3 tablespoons butter

Apple Topping

2 apples

1 tablespoon butter

1 teaspoon sugar

1 teaspoon cinnamon

1 teaspoon powdered sugar

Directions

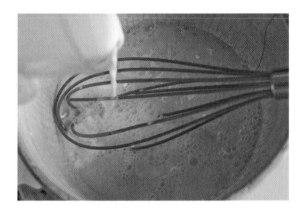

1. Place the skillet in the oven and preheat to 425°. Once the oven is hot, whisk the eggs in the mixing bowl to lighten them. Whisk in the milk. Sprinkle the flour into the milk mixture and continue whisking for a minute, until almost all of the lumps disappear.

2. Carefully put three tablespoons of butter into a hot skillet and tilt the pan so the bottom is coated. Pour in batter and tilt the pan again to spread the batter evenly. Bake for 20 minutes, until golden brown and puffy. Don't open the oven for the first 15 minutes of baking.

3. While the puffcake is in the oven, melt remaining butter, sugar, and cinnamon over medium-low heat in the other skillet. Peel and thinly slice the apples, and then add them to the pan. Cook the apples, stirring frequently, until they are tender. Remove from the heat and set aside.

NOTE

Getting the proper "puff" from oven pancakes requires the right size and type of pan, which should be preheated in the oven for best results—but only if it's sturdy metal, like cast iron. When the batter is poured into the hot pan, the butter helps it slide up the sides as it inflates and cooks.

Caution: A cast iron skillet retains heat for a long time, so make sure the hot skillet is away from the edge of counter where kids might reach for it.

---

4. When the puffcake is done, remove it from the oven and place it on a heatproof surface. Scoop the apples into the middle and dust them with powdered sugar. Serve immediately. Cut the puffcake into wedges after it is on the table so it doesn't deflate before everyone gets a chance to see it.

Eggs Berkeley

S HARP CHEDDAR CHEESE and the mild onion flavor of chives lend bright flavor to gently scrambled eggs in this, the signature egg dish of The Inn at Lucky Mud (luckymud.com). Served with a slice of whole-grain toast and some fresh fruit, these eggs make a nutritious breakfast that you can make in just 10 minutes.

Serves 2

Active Time: 10 minutes

Total Time: 10 minutes

Tools: Mixing bowl, whisk, skillet, and spatula

Nutritional Information per Serving: 244 Calories; 19g Fat (70.0% calories from fat); 17g Protein; 1g Carbohydrate; trace Dietary Fiber; 354mg Cholesterol; 550mg Sodium

Ingredients

3 eggs

1 tablespoon cream (or milk)

1/4 teaspoon salt

2 tablespoons chives

1/2 cup shredded sharp cheddar cheese

Directions

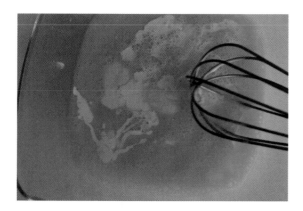

1. Break eggs into a bowl and whisk briefly to break up. Add the cream and salt and beat until well blended and somewhat airy. (You can also use a blender, pulsing it a few times until everything is well mixed.)

3. Sprinkle on cheese and chives. Cook for another 30-60 seconds, to desired degree of doneness. Serve immediately.

2. Heat butter in a skillet over medium heat. Pour eggs into the skillet and cook, pulling the cooked eggs from the outside of the pan towards the center, until the eggs lose most of their moisture.

Orange Glazed Bacon

B AKED IN THE OVEN this sweet and sour glazed bacon is easy to make, requires no attention once it is in the oven, and won't splatter hot grease on anyone.

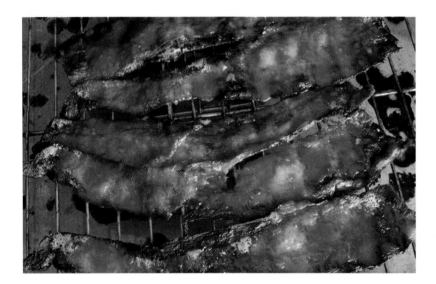

Serves 4

Active Time: 5 minutes

Total Time: 20 minutes

Tools: Small bowl, brush, baking sheet (with sides), and cake rack

Nutritional Information per Serving: 81 Calories; 6g Fat (70.4% calories from fat); 4g Protein; 2g Carbohydrate; trace Dietary Fiber; 11mg Cholesterol; 288mg Sodium

Ingredients

1 tablespoon frozen orange juice concentrate, thawed

1 teaspoon soy sauce

8 slices bacon

Directions

1. Preheat oven to 400°. Place rack on baking sheet. Stir the orange juice concentrate and soy sauce together in a small bowl.

3. Brush the bacon with the glaze. Bake for about 10-15 minutes, depending on thickness of bacon, until crisp. Serve immediately.

2. Lay the strips of bacon out on the rack.

Coconut Almond Granola

THIS CRUNCHY CEREAL is rich and nutty, providing a perfect background for dried fruit that you add when it is served. High in fiber, iron, and thiamin as well as quite a bit lower in fat than the typical granola from the store, it has the nutritional punch to get you through a busy morning. Mix in dried fruit when you serve it to maintain the cereal's crispness.

Makes about 6 cups

Active Time: 15 minutes

Total Time: 60-90 minutes

Tools: Small bowl, mixing spoon, mixing bowl, cookie sheet, and spatula

Nutritional Information per 1/2 Cup Serving: 287 Calories; 13g Fat (38.9% calories from fat); 9g Protein; 36g Carbohydrate; 6g Dietary Fiber; 0mg Cholesterol; 12mg Sodium

Ingredients

2 cups quick-cooking oats (not instant)

3/4 cup oat flour (see page 52)

1/2 cup wheat germ

1/2 cup flax seed, ground

3/4 cup sliced almonds

1/3 cup sesame seeds

1/2 cup coconut

1/2 cup frozen apple juice concentrate, thawed

1/4 cup maple syrup

1/2 teaspoon cinnamon

1/2 tablespoon nutmeg

Directions

1. Preheat oven to 300°. Stir the oatmeal, wheat germ, flax seed, oat bran, almonds, sesame seeds, and coconut together in a large bowl.

2. Stir the juice concentrate, maple syrup, cinnamon, and nutmeg together in a small bowl. Pour over the dry ingredients and mix together well.

3. Spread the granola on the baking sheet, squeezing small clumps together. Bake for 30 minutes and then remove from the oven and stir. Bake for another 20 minutes and stir again. Continue baking and stirring, 10 minutes at a time, until the granola is a golden brown and all of the moisture is absorbed.

4. Let the granola cool completely on pan. Break up any overly large clusters into bite-sized pieces. Store in a tightly sealed container at room temperature for up to a month.

Try This: Blending Your Own Granola

This is just one possible blend of ingredients for granola. You can make your own blend of granola using almost any cereal grain, nuts, and seeds as long as you maintain a couple of basic ratios, both based on volume. Use eight parts dry ingredients to one part wet. Seeds and nuts should be 25-50% of the total dry ingredients.

Too Cool for School Breakfast Parfaits

FRUIT LAYERED WITH RICH, CREAMY YOGURT and a bit of granola for crunch makes for a tempting and healthful breakfast. High in protein, fiber, calcium, and lots of other essential vitamins and nutrients, this is a great start to a busy day.

Serves 1

Active Time: 5 minutes

Total Time: 5 minutes

Tools: Knife and spoon

Nutritional Information per Serving

Strawberry Banana Parfait: 327 Calories; 7g Fat (19.8% calories from fat); 20g Protein; 48g Carbohydrate; 7g Dietary Fiber; 4mg Cholesterol; 195mg Sodium

Mango Blueberry Parfait: 374 Calories; 7g Fat (17.1% calories from fat); 20g Protein; 61g Carbohydrate; 7g Dietary Fiber; 4mg Cholesterol; 199mg Sodium

Ingredients

1 cup non-fat vanilla yogurt

1 cup strawberries (or your fruit of choice), sliced

1/4 cup Coconut Almond Granola (see page 78)

1 teaspoon brown sugar

Fresh mint leaves, for garnish (optional)

Directions

1. Stir the yogurt and cinnamon together in a small bowl. (You can make a quantity of this ahead of time and store, tightly covered, in the refrigerator, until the yogurt's "use by" date.)

2. Place about half of the fruit in a bowl or tall glass. Spoon half of the yogurt on top of the fruit. Sprinkle with half of the granola.

3. Repeat with another layer of fruit, yogurt, and granola, reserving just a little yogurt and a few bits of fruit for the top.

4. Top with the last dollop of yogurt and pieces of fruit. Garnish with mint. Serve immediately.

Rise and Shine Ham and Cheese Strata

CLASSIC HAM AND EGGS meets an old-fashioned breakfast casserole in this warm and filling breakfast. This quick version is made like a savory bread pudding, rather than the traditional layers that gave this dish its name. Make it the night before and bake it up in the morning for an easy Saturday breakfast or a fancy holiday brunch.

Serves 8

Active Time: 10 minutes

Total Time: Overnight

Tools: 9×13 baking dish, mixing bowl, whisk, and aluminum foil

Nutritional Information per Serving: 255 Calories; 15g Fat (52.3% calories from fat); 16g Protein; 13g Carbohydrate; trace Dietary Fiber; 198mg Cholesterol; 640mg Sodium

Ingredients

6 slices bread, torn into bite-sized pieces

6 ounces ham, cut into 1/2" cubes

1 1/4 cups shredded cheddar cheese, divided

2 tablespoons chives, snipped into small pieces

6 eggs

2 cups milk

1/4 teaspoon salt

1/2 teaspoon ground pepper

1/2 tablespoon dry mustard

Directions

1. Mix the bread, ham, chives, and one cup of the cheese together in the 9×13 baking dish.

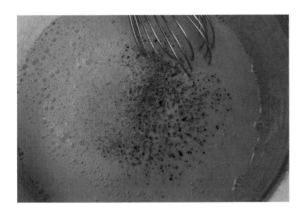

2. Whisk the eggs to lighten. Mix in the milk, salt, pepper, and mustard.

3. Pour the eggs over the bread. Sprinkle with the remaining 1/4 cup cheese. Cover tightly with foil and refrigerate overnight.

4. Remove the strata from the refrigerator about an hour before baking. Preheat oven to 350°. Bake uncovered 50-60 minutes, until golden brown and puffed up. If needed, place foil loosely on the top to prevent overbrowning. Let rest 5-10 minutes before serving.

Try This:
Stratas Made Your Way

Almost any type of vegetable or meat can go into a strata, making them a great way to use leftovers. Before adding vegetables with a high water content, like onions or zucchini, sauté them briefly to remove some of the moisture.

Light and Fluffy Oat Pancakes

THE NUTTY FLAVOR OF OATMEAL, always a breakfast favorite, shows up in an unexpected place: pancakes. High in fiber, protein, and vitamins B1 and B2, these pancakes are great topped with fruit and a dusting of powdered sugar or classic maple syrup.

Serves 2 (6-8 pancakes)

Active Time: 10 minutes

Total Time: 20 minutes

Tools: Mixing bowl, whisk, spatula, griddle or large, and flat frying pan

Nutritional Information per Serving: 275 Calories; 5g Fat (17.2% calories from fat); 15g Protein; 44g Carbohydrate; 6g Dietary Fiber; 110mg Cholesterol; 833mg Sodium

Ingredients

1/2 cup oat flour (see page 52)

1/2 cup whole wheat flour

1 teaspoon sugar

1 teaspoon baking powder

1/4 teaspoon baking soda

1/4 teaspoon salt

1 egg

1 cup buttermilk (or mix 1 teaspoon vinegar and 1 cup milk)

Directions

1. Stir dry ingredients together. Mix ingredients together in a separate bowl until well-combined. Slowly whisk dry ingredients into wet until just incorporated. You may need to add another tablespoon or two of milk for the right consistency. For thicker, fluffier pancakes, let the batter rest for 15-30 minutes and do not stir again before cooking.

2. Spray the pan with non-stick spray or brush with a smidge of butter. Pour batter onto pan a scant 1/4 cup at a time. When you can see bubbles pop through the top of the pancake, flip them over and cook for another minute or so. Serve with warm maple syrup, fresh fruit, or other favorite pancake toppings.

Cook's Tip

A test pancake is a quick way to make sure the griddle is the right temperature. Pour a tablespoonful of batter on the hot griddle and watch for the bubbles that indicate it is ready to flip. They should appear in about 1 1/2-2 minutes, slightly less time than with a regular sized pancake. Adjust the cooking temperature as needed.

Cook's Tip

Freeze pancakes for almost instant breakfasts. After cooking, cool pancakes, wrap tightly in plastic, and freeze in a freezer bag. Remove as many pancakes as you need and heat in a microwave or toaster oven.

Bananas for Breakfast!

THESE BANANAS are unabashedly a treat, with bits of crisped sugar on the meltingly warm exterior. Serve these with any of your favorite breakfast foods or, for an indulgence, include a stack of "Light and Fluff Oat Pancakes" with them.

Serves 1

Active Time: 10 minutes

Total Time: 10 minutes

Tools: Knife, skillet, and spatula

Nutritional Information per Serving: 156 Calories; 4g Fat (23.3% calories from fat); 1g Protein; 31g Carbohydrate; 3g Dietary Fiber; 10mg Cholesterol; 41mg Sodium

Ingredients

1 banana

1 teaspoon butter

2 teaspoon Cinnayum! Sugar (see the "Try This!" sidebar)

Directions

1. Peel the banana and lay it down on the counter. Slice in half lengthwise to make two long curving pieces. (If a small child will be helping, you may want to cut each piece in half to make them easier to work with.)

3. Flip the bananas and sprinkle the rest of the sugar on top of them. Cook for a few more minutes, until the edges of the banana soften and brown.

Try This:
Cinnayum! Adds Spice

Replace predictable cinnamon sugar with flavorful Cinnayum! Sugar, which adds brown sugar and spices to the traditional mix. The recipe for Cinnayum! Sugar is on page 53.

2. Heat a skillet on medium heat. When it is hot, add the butter and swirl to melt. Lay banana halves in the pan cut side down and sprinkle half of the sugar over them. Cook for 2-3 minutes, until the banana starts to get crispy and the sugar on top of the banana starts to dissolve.

4

The

Lunchbox

Photos courtesy
Sarah Jackson Photography

WHETHER YOU ARE brown-bagging it or enjoying a leisurely weekend at home, lunch can be more fun than you might think. Whereas schooldays are a good time for old favorites, weekends offer a bit more time to explore new things.

Most of the recipes in this chapter can be sent to school or used as the foundation for a more elaborate lunch at home. Recipes like salmon patties, turkey kabobs, butternut squash soup, and black bean and sweet potato stew can be made ahead of time and frozen for easy school-day lunches.

Marvelous Midday Meals

LUNCH IS A VASTLY underrated meal. It is, in fact two entirely different meals, depending on what day it is. During the week, brown-bagging to school or office means that each meal has to please only one person. If you want the same sandwich every day for a week, or a month, that's your prerogative when it's a meal made for one. Lunches for one are also a good time for those things that only one person likes.

Weekend lunches, on the other hand, are little like weekdays—where the goal is a quick, easy and reliably-liked meal to be eaten away from home. Weekends give you time to play with your food and experiment with new dishes. Compared to dinner, there are few time constraints, so you can choose dishes that take a little longer. Because it is not the main meal of the day, ingredients tend to be less expensive and people's expectations are different, so a less than stellar experiment is not a major tragedy.

Schooldays, however, are not usually the best time for untested menu items. Kids have little time to eat and the only fallback is trading items they don't like with other students (which they do, even when it is forbidden due to concerns about allergies) or skipping lunch entirely. Rather than send a new, untried recipe to school and risk a missed lunch—never a good idea with children who have to work hard in class—pick a weekend day every once in a while to try new meals with your child.

School lunches don't have to be complicated. A favorite sandwich or thermos of soup and some fruit will often do. Jot down a list of tried and true lunch options for those days when you just can't think of a thing to make. Prepare lunch ahead of time as much as possible. A good time is in the evening, while dinner is cooking or before cleaning up after the meal. You will not make much more mess and may even be able combine preparation steps, like cleaning and chopping vegetables.

Lunch preparation should be a family affair. Your kids should help make their lunch, just like other meals. Also, letting children help make their own lunches means they are more likely to eat it.

Even though school lunch is often casual, don't forget to have a good time with it. Here are a few tips to help you make school lunches interesting:

- **Change your approach**—If brown-bagging it usually means sandwiches, try a lunch of finger food. A thermos of hot soup is a welcome option on a December day. Even changing from regular sandwich bread to pita or crackers can make a big difference in what lunch tastes like.

- **Have fun**—Pick a silly idea and build a lunch around it: a single color of food, things a cowboy would eat, food from a favorite movie, and so on. Your only limit is your imagination.

- **Include a treat, like a single bite of chocolate or even a small bag of favored fruit**—The first cherries of the season can be as indulgent as dessert! Don't forget the occasional non-food treat, too. An encouraging note on the day of a test or just a sticky note with a smile and "I love you!" can add a special smile to your child's lunch.

CAUTION

Severe peanut allergies are showing up in so many kids that some schools have banned peanuts entirely. This means that even if your child isn't allergic, you can't send any food with peanuts in their lunch. If you can send peanuts to school, wait until your children are old enough to understand that, while trading lunches can be fun, peanuts can't be traded with certain kids.

Just like with food served at home, what a school lunch looks like makes a difference to your child, starting with the lunchbox. There is a seemingly endless selection of containers to use when carting lunch about, and letting your children pick their own means they will be happy to carry it to school every day.

▶ **Get the right lunchbox for your child**—It should be easy to carry, large enough for their typical lunch, and attractive. Look for metal or plastic. Avoid vinyl, as some vinyl has been found to contain lead.

▶ **Make sure that you have insulated containers for soup and other hot items**—Preheat them with hot water before packing so the food stays warm longer.

▶ **Small freezer packs come in kid-friendly colors and designs**—Alternatively, you can freeze part of lunch itself, like a juice box. By lunch time, it will be ready to eat but the rest of lunch will stay cool in the meantime.

▶ **Get supplies**—Tiny containers for dip and sauce; bright washcloths for napkins; you can even buy a washable fabric sandwich wrapper.

Figure 4.1
Choose reusable lunch supplies to keep a lot of trash out of the landfill.
Photo courtesy Sarah Jackson Photography

Note

It has been estimated that a child using disposable lunch packaging will generate 67 pounds of waste over the course of a year, at a cost of almost $250. This is a quite a bit of waste and expense, both of which can be eliminated with a moderate one-time expenditure.

Shopping Help!

A collection of links to cool lunchboxes and supplies are posted at this book's website:

blog.cookingwithyourkids.net/bookLinks.html

Skamokawa Salmon Burger

SKAMOKAWA (Skuh-MOCK-away), a tiny fishing hamlet on the Columbia River in Washington, is home to some of the best wild salmon in the world. Mix canned salmon with bits of sweet red pepper and crunchy celery for a fresh take on salmon patties. Make a tasty sandwich for a school lunchbox using tarragon mayonnaise, tomato, and lettuce slipped into a pita bread. In addition to being a great source of omega-3 fatty acids, these salmon patties are high in protein, calcium, and vitamin B6, and have 70% of the B12 you need in a day.

Makes 3 patties

Active Time: 15 minutes

Total Time: 15 minutes

Tools: Mixing bowl, skillet, and spatula

Nutritional Information per Serving: 175 Calories; 10g Fat (51.2% calories from fat); 15g Protein; 7g Carbohydrate; 1g Dietary Fiber; 102mg Cholesterol; 548mg Sodium

Ingredients

6 ounces canned salmon (no salt added), drained and flaked

1 egg, lightly beaten

1/3 cup panko bread crumbs

2 scallions, chopped

1 stalk celery, chopped

1 tablespoon red pepper, chopped fine (optional)

1 tablespoon fresh parsley, chopped

1/4 teaspoon salt

1/4 teaspoon pepper

1/2 lemon zest

1 tablespoon olive oil

Directions

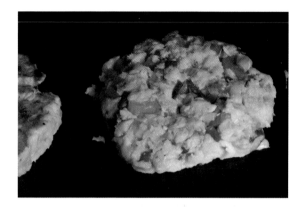

1. Mix together salmon, egg, panko, scallions, celery, red pepper, and lemon zest in a bowl. Use a spoon or let the kids do it with clean hands.

2. Gently form two patties, about 1/2 inch thick. You can make ahead to this point and store, tightly covered, in the refrigerator for 24 hours.

3. Heat the olive oil in the skillet over medium to medium-high heat. Place the patties in the pan and cook for 3-4 minutes, until the bottom is browned. Flip the patties and cook another 3-4 minutes. Serve immediately or let cool and serve at room temperature. Cooked patties can be kept in the refrigerator for several days.

Tarragon Mayonnaise

1/3 cup mayonnaise

3 tablespoons yogurt

1 clove garlic, minced

1 teaspoon fresh tarragon (1/2 teaspoon dried)

1 teaspoon lemon juice

Mix all ingredients in a small bowl. Let flavors mingle for at least 30 minutes before serving, refrigerate if it will be longer than that before serving. Keeps in the refrigerator until about the yogurt's pull date.

Crunchy Chicken Cranberry Pockets

S WEET DRIED CRANBERRIES and crunchy almond slivers give this chicken salad its character. Pita bread helps contain the inevitable, and tasty, mess of chicken salad sandwiches. This is a great use for small amounts of leftover chicken or turkey. This recipe makes one generous sandwich; you might want to send a half as lunch for younger kids.

Serves 1

Active Time: 5 minutes

Total Time: 5 minutes

Tools: Mixing bowl and spoon

Nutritional Information per Serving: 633 Calories; 28g Fat (38.1% calories from fat); 37g Protein; 66g Carbohydrate; 9g Dietary Fiber; 77mg Cholesterol; 528mg Sodium

Ingredients

5 ounces chicken, cubed

1 stalk celery, chopped

1 tablespoon sliced almonds

2 tablespoons dried cranberries

1 tablespoon mayonnaise

1 pinch salt

1 whole wheat pita bread

Handful of lettuce leaves

Directions

1. Mix chicken, celery, almonds, cranberries, mayonnaise, and salt in a bowl.

2. Cut the pita in half and gently open the pocket with your hands. Put some lettuce in each half of the pita. Divide the filling between the pita halves, putting it between the layers of lettuce to keep the bread from getting soggy before lunchtime.

Cooking Meat Safely

To be safest, cook meat to these internal temperatures at a minimum. Beef, veal, and lamb should be cooked 160°. Poultry should be cooked to 165°. Seafood should be cooked to 145°. Pork should be cooked to 160°.

CAUTION

Remember to be very careful working with hot water around children. Wait until you are convinced that your children can safely deal with boiling water before you let them handle it.

Pasta Primavera Salad

THIS LIGHT DISH, full of late summer vegetable bounty, is great for summer lunches or those unexpectedly warm fall days. The ingredients are flexible so you can mix and match alternate vegetables as you prefer; just chop them into bite-sized pieces. This recipe is a lifelong favorite of Ryan MacMichael, who writes about all things vegan at vegblog.org.

Serves 8

Active Time: 20 minutes

Total Time: 1 1/2 hours

Tools: Mixing bowl, large spoon, small bowl, and whisk

Nutritional Information per Serving: 279 Calories; 16g Fat (49.6% calories from fat); 6g Protein; 31g Carbohydrate; 5g Dietary Fiber; 0mg Cholesterol; 159mg Sodium

Ingredients

8 ounces whole wheat spaghetti, cooked and drained

4 medium tomatoes, peeled and chopped (see the "Peeling a Tomato" sidebar)

1 medium cucumber, chopped

1 small green pepper, seeded and chopped (1/2" cubes)

1 small onion, chopped

1 cup black olives, chopped

1/4 cup fresh parsley (1 1/2 tablespoon dried)

1 small zucchini, chopped (1/2" cubes)

Salt to taste

Dressing

1/2 cup extra virgin olive oil

1 tablespoon sugar

3 tablespoons white wine (see Note)

2 teaspoons lemon juice

1 tablespoon fresh basil (1 teaspoon dried)

1/4 teaspoon pepper

1 dash Tabasco sauce

Directions

1. Whisk the olive oil, sugar, wine, lemon juice, basil, pepper, and Tabasco sauce together in a small bowl.

2. Combine tomatoes, cucumber, green pepper, onion, olives, parsley, spaghetti, zucchini and tofu feta in a bowl and stir to mix the ingredients. Drizzle the dressing over the salad and gently stir to coat. Refrigerate at least an hour to let the flavors mellow before serving.

Note

Although the amount of alcohol in a single serving is negligible, you can substitute alcohol-free wine or mild vinegar if you prefer.

Peeling a Tomato

Fill a mixing bowl with ice water and set it aside. Bring a saucepan of water to a boil. (You can use the pasta water before you cook the pasta and do several tomatoes at a time, as long as the pan and bowl will hold them without spilling.) Use tongs or a slotted spoon to gently lower a tomato into the boiling water for 30 seconds. Remove the tomato from the boiling water and plunge it into the ice water immediately to stop it from cooking. After a few seconds, remove the tomato from the water; the skin will peel off easily. To remove the seeds, tear or cut the tomato in half and scrape the gooey parts out with your fingers—a perfect job for the kids!

Try This: Pasta Variations

Leave out the olives, as Ryan does, or use his mom's favorite, steamed broccoli, instead of the zucchini.

Add 1 cup of tofu feta and omit the salt. You can purchase tofu cheese in health food stores and most supermarkets or, if you are feeling adventurous, even make your own. Homemade tofu cheese is simple to make and kids have a great time making it. Some recipes for tofu feta can be found here: blog.cookingwithyourkids. net/bookLinks.html.

Black Bean and Sweet Potato Stew

THIS EARTHY, SPICY STEW is delicious for lunch on a chilly fall day. You can add any extra vegetables you have on hand, bits of meat (sausage is an excellent addition), and make it spicy, or not, as you like. High in fiber, protein, and vitamin C, and with more than a day's worth of vitamin A, you might want to make extra to freeze and reheat.

Serves 6

Active Time: 15 minutes

Total Time: 1 hour 20 minutes

Tools: High-sided skillet or Dutch oven, spatula

Nutritional Information per Serving: 261 Calories; 8g Fat (27.9% calories from fat); 13g Protein; 36g Carbohydrate; 10g Dietary Fiber; 9mg Cholesterol; 480mg Sodium

Ingredients

1 medium onion, peeled and chopped

1 tablespoon olive oil

2 stalks celery, sliced 1/2" thick

2 15-ounce can black beans, drained and rinsed

2 medium sweet potatoes, peeled and cut into 2"cubes (about 1-1 1/4 pound)

2 cups no-salt-added chicken broth

2 cloves garlic, minced

1/4 teaspoon cumin

1/2 teaspoon allspice

1/4 teaspoon cayenne (optional)

2 bay leaves

1/2 cup sour cream

1/4 cup chives, snipped

Directions

1. Heat olive oil in pan over medium heat. Add onions and cook, stirring occasionally, for about 5 minutes, until they relax and start to turn translucent. Add celery and cook for 3-4 minutes, until it becomes aromatic.

2. Add the black beans, sweet potato, stock, garlic, cumin, allspice, cayenne, and bay leaf to the pan. Cover, turn down heat to medium-low and simmer about 30 minutes, until the sweet potatoes are tender and the sauce is thickened and flavorful. Serve in individual bowls, topped with a dollop of sour cream and a sprinkling of chives.

**Try This:
Spicy Sausage**

Slice some spicy sausage, like Andouille or Chorizo, and add it to the pan after the celery. Cook for a few minutes, until the meat browns a little, and then proceed with the rest of the recipe.

Gobble It Up Turkey Kabobs

TURKEY AND BROWN RICE come together with savory sautéed vegetables and herbs in these miniature meatballs. Skewers of meatballs and your favorite fresh vegetables, brushed with a sweet and savory glaze, can go to school with the kids. Make a double batch and grill kabobs over the barbeque for a healthful alternative to hot dogs and burgers.

Serves 4

Active Time: 30 minutes

Total Time: 45 minutes

Tools: Skillet, mixing bowl, baking sheet, skewers, and brush

Nutritional Information per Serving: 294 Calories; 11g Fat (34.3% calories from fat); 25g Protein; 22g Carbohydrate; 1g Dietary Fiber; 119mg Cholesterol; 354mg Sodium

Ingredients

Meatballs
1 pound ground turkey (look for low-fat)

1 teaspoon olive oil

1/2 small onion, chopped fine

1 stalk celery, chopped fine

1 cup brown rice, cooked

1 egg, beaten slightly

1 tablespoon chopped fresh sage

1/4 teaspoon ground black pepper

1/2 teaspoon salt

Basting Sauce
2 tablespoons balsamic vinegar

2 tablespoons honey

1 teaspoon olive oil

For Kabobs
Your choice of fresh summer vegetables like zucchini, peppers, onions, mushrooms, and so on. Cut in pieces about the same size as the meatballs, and parboil if necessary. (To *parboil*, cook ingredients in a pot of boiling water until mostly done. Potatoes, for example, should be cooked until you can easily slide a knife in just a little before it meets resistance.)

Directions

1. Preheat oven to 400°. If you are using wooden skewers, put them into a pan of water to soak. Cook onions and celery in olive oil in skillet over medium heat for about five minutes, until the onion wilts and becomes translucent. Place in the mixing bowl with the turkey, rice, egg, sage, salt, and pepper. Mix well. Divide the meat into four parts. Working with one quarter at a time, shape into four balls.

2. Thread meatballs onto skewers, alternating with vegetables. Place the skewers on a baking sheet. Mix the balsamic vinegar, honey, and olive oil together in a small bowl, and then brush it on the skewers. Bake for about 15 minutes, turning once, until the meatballs are golden brown. Alternatively, grill over medium-hot coals for 10-12 minutes.

Note

There are two ways to make this for the lunchbox.

► Freeze a batch of raw meatballs. Thaw meatballs and cook skewers in the evening for school lunch the next day.

► Freeze cooked meatballs and defrost overnight in refrigerator. When the meatballs are thawed enough, put on skewers alternating with ready to eat chunks of raw or blanched vegetables your children enjoys.

Pack a small container of marinara or low-fat salad dressing for dipping.

Seriously Good Stuffed Tomatoes

THIS AMERICAN CLASSIC is updated with feta and capers by Kevin Weeks, a personal chef and food writer from Knoxville, Tennessee (seriouslygood.kdweeks.com). Kevin says just the smell of fresh tomatoes can take him back to days of eating this childhood favorite at the kitchen counter. These tomatoes are high in protein, vitamins C, A, B6, B12, and niacin.

Serves 4

Active Time: 10 minutes

Total Time: 1 hour 10 minutes

Tools: Small knife, mixing bowl, and spoon

Nutritional Information per Serving: 231 Calories; 15g Fat (56.4% calories from fat); 14g Protein; 12g Carbohydrate; 2g Dietary Fiber; 26mg Cholesterol; 456mg Sodium

Ingredients

4 large tomatoes, 3" diameter

1 6-oz can water-packed tuna, drained

8 Saltine crackers, crushed

1/4 cup scallions, sliced into 1/8" rounds

1/4 cup green pepper, diced

2 tablespoon capers

1/4 cup feta cheese, crumbled

2 tablespoons feta brine

1/2 lemon, juiced

1/4 cup mayonnaise

1/4 teaspoon cayenne pepper

Directions

1. Remove tomato tops and dice. Remove pulp from tomatoes, discard seeds, and dice flesh. Place diced pulp in mixing bowl. Cover whole tomatoes and leave on the counter; refrigerating changes the flavor.

2. Combine tomato, tuna, crackers, scallions, green pepper, capers, feta cheese, feta brine, lemon juice, mayonnaise, and cayenne pepper in a bowl. Cover and allow flavors to meld for 1 hour. To serve, sprinkle a little salt on the insides of tomatoes and stuff with tuna mixture. Serve immediately.

Cook's Tip

If your feta comes without brine, you can use lemon juice instead.

Squish Squash Soup

S MOOTH AND RICH, this soup can be made in less than an hour, and with any kind of winter squash. The (optional) addition of a little cream transforms this simple soup from everyday fare into a truly special dish. This simple to make soup is high in fiber, protein, potassium, vitamins C, A, B1, B6, folacin, and niacin with only a trace of fat.

Serves 6

Active Time: 15 minutes

Total Time: 45-60 minutes

Tools: Saucepan, wooden spoon, vegetable peeler or paring knife, and (optional) potato masher or immersion blender

Nutrition per One Cup Serving: 188 Calories; trace Fat (1.6% calories from fat); 9g Protein; 43g Carbohydrate; 7g Dietary Fiber; 0mg Cholesterol; 273mg Sodium

With Cream: 237 Calories; 5g Fat (18.6% calories from fat); 9g Protein; 43g Carbohydrate; 7g Dietary Fiber; 17mg Cholesterol; 280mg Sodium

Ingredients

1 medium butternut squash

1 large russet potato

3 cups low sodium chicken broth

1 cup apple juice

2 bay leaves

1 teaspoon fresh sage, finely minced (or 1/2 teaspoon dried sage)

1/4 teaspoon ground cayenne pepper

1/2 cup cream (optional)

Directions

1. Cut the butternut squash in half crosswise and then peel it with a vegetable peeler or paring knife. Cut the rounded end in half, and then scrape out the seeds and discard them. Cut the squash into roughly 2" pieces. Peel the potato and cut it in similar sized chunks. (Your child can cut the potato, if not the squash, with a plastic knife.)

2. Place chicken stock, squash, potato, and apple juice in a large saucepan and cook over medium heat, stirring occasionally, for 30-40 minutes, until you can easily mash the squash and potato with the spoon.

3. Remove the pan from the heat, remove the bay leaves, and mash the squash and potatoes completely with a wooden spoon, potato masher, or immersion blender. (Keep the immersion blender on a low speed so the hot liquid doesn't splash you.)

4. Return the pan to medium heat, stir in the cayenne, and bring to a simmer. Taste and add more cayenne, if needed. You may also need salt, particularly if you are using homemade stock. If you are using cream: Just before serving, stir in most of the cream, reserving a few teaspoons to drizzle on top once it is in bowls. (You can freeze this soup after it cools, but don't add cream if you are planning on doing so.)

Chef's unSalad Wraps

THIS DECONSTRUCTED CHEF'S SALAD is rolled into a long cylinder and dipped into creamy dressing. Because it takes only a small amount of any individual ingredient, it is a tasty way to use up leftovers and odds and ends. Add some whole grain crackers or a breadstick for an easy finger food lunch that is high in fiber, protein, calcium, vitamins C, A, B1, B2, B6, B12, and folacin.

Serves 1

Active Time: 10 minutes

Total Time: 10 minutes

Tools: Knife and frilled toothpicks (optional)

Nutritional Information per Serving, Including Dressing: 300 Calories; 16g Fat (46.0% calories from fat); 23g Protein; 18g Carbohydrate; 5g Dietary Fiber; 241mg Cholesterol; 672mg Sodium

Ingredients

1 cup soft leafy lettuce

1 ounce low-fat Swiss cheese, cut into matchsticks

1 ounce ham, cut into matchsticks

1 hard-boiled egg, sliced into lengthwise wedges

1 carrot, cut into matchsticks

1 stalk celery, cut into matchsticks

1/2 small cucumber, cut into matchsticks and seeded

1 ounce (2 tablespoons) Creamy Herb dressing (see page 172), or other dressing of your choice

Directions

1. Lay a piece of lettuce on the counter. Put a few pieces of meat, cheese, egg, and vegetables on the lettuce. Roll up and stick a toothpick through the middle to hold it together. Repeat with the rest of the ingredients, using different combinations of fillings. Serve the dressing on the side for dipping.

Cook's Tip

When choosing lettuce for this unSalad, pick something that has leaves at least 4-5 inches long and soft enough to roll it up like a straw. Leaf and butterhead (or bibb) lettuce are good choices, as is young romaine. Mature romaine and crisp head lettuce, like iceberg, does not roll very well.

Try This: Wraps Your Way

The possible variations on this dish are endless. Here are a few ideas to get you started:

▶ Replace the ham and cheddar cheese with turkey and smoked gouda, and then add some halved seedless red grapes.

▶ Add small (grape or cherry) tomatoes, halved or quartered. Remove and discard watery seeds.

▶ Include a small handful of sunflower seeds or slivered almonds to dip the rolls in after the dressing.

Ants in an Apple!

S END SOMETHING UNEXPECTED to school for lunch, like this apple, which is an optical illusion. It looks whole but it is actually cored and cut in wedges, and then reassembled with kid favorites—peanut butter and raisins in the core. Add a handful of edamame (ready-to-eat soybeans in their pods) and some crackers to round out a finger food meal.

Serves 1

Active Time: 5 minutes

Total Time: 5 minutes

Tools: Knife, small bowl, spoon, and plastic wrap

Nutritional Information per Serving: 458 Calories; 25g Fat (45.4% calories from fat); 14g Protein; 54g Carbohydrate; 7g Dietary Fiber; 0mg Cholesterol; 233mg Sodium

Ingredients

1 ounce peanut butter

1/4 cup raisins

1 Granny Smith apple

Directions

1. Put the peanut butter in a small bowl and stir it to loosen. Stir in raisins.

2. Cut apple in quarters lengthwise. Slice the core off diagonally. With the skin side down, cut each quarter into several wedges, leaving a little skin attached to hold the wedges together.

3. Hold two quarters of the apple in the palm of one hand. Scoop the peanut butter into the hollow of the apple. Reassemble the apple with the other two quarters. Wrap tightly in plastic.

Try This:
Other Kinds of Nut Butter

You can also use other kinds of nut butter. Almond, soy nut, macadamia, and sunflower seed butters are also very tasty.

Magic Microwave Mac 'n Cheese

ALTHOUGH MANY PEOPLE think of macaroni and cheese as a staple only of childhood, lots of adults consider it to be perfect comfort food, too. It is simple to make from scratch, even by a child armed with only a microwave. The magic in this recipe is what happens in the last few minutes in the microwave when a soup with some uncooked pasta suddenly transforms into a rich, creamy casserole. Try this recipe and you'll stop buying boxes with dried cheese powder.

Serves 4

Active Time: 5 minutes

Total Time: 15 minutes

Tools: 1 quart covered microwave baking dish, spoon, and microwave

Nutritional Information per One Cup Serving: 414 Calories; 17g Fat (35.0% calories from fat); 22g Protein; 47g Carbohydrate; 5g Dietary Fiber; 51mg Cholesterol; 453mg Sodium

Ingredients

8 ounces whole grain pasta

3 cups water

1 1/2 cups low-fat milk

1/4 teaspoon salt

1 1/2 cups (6 ounces) shredded sharp cheddar cheese

Directions

1. Place pasta in microwave-safe baking dish. Pour water and milk over the pasta, and sprinkle on the salt. Stir to mix. Cover and microwave on high for 12-15 minutes, stopping to stir twice, until the pasta is just short of tender. (Note that up until about 60 seconds before it is done cooking, this looks like watery soup with uncooked noodles. Have faith, the magic works.)

2. Stir in the cheese. Cook for another 1-2 minutes, until the cheese is melted. Remove from the microwave and stir. Cover and let stand for a few minutes before serving.

Cook's Tip

This can also be prepared in a conventional oven. After mixing the ingredients in step 1, bake at 350° for 25-30 minutes, until the pasta is almost done cooking. Stir in the cheese and continue baking another 5-10 minutes, until the cheese is melted. If you like the top to form a bit of a crunchy crust, leave it uncovered when you add the cheese.

5

The
Main Dish

THE THOUGHT OF A FAMILY DINNER, with peaceful children happily eating a balanced meal while chattering about their day, is an appealing ideal. The reality, however, is that, between the demands of work and their overscheduled kids, many parents consider themselves lucky to get a slice of tomato on their kid's drive-through burger.

Resist the siren song of the drive-through window with the recipes in this chapter, which range from kid-tested favorites such as pasta and meatballs with fresh marinara salsa to a simple soufflé. All of these meals can be on the table in about an hour—even the homemade pizza crust can be made the night before for a quick after-work pizza dinner. There are also a few tips about getting from the door to the dinner table with a minimum of stress.

Family Dinner Matters

IT SEEMS OBVIOUS when you think about it: family dinner matters.

Most importantly, it gives your family a time to reconnect at the end of an often hectic and scattered day. Dinnertime can be full of laughter and good food, building the foundation for treasured family memories. Conversations around the dinner table offer you a chance to hear what matters to your kids. This is particularly useful as kids get older, spend more time away from home—and often don't want to talk much even if they are sitting right there with you!

Figure 5.1
Kids can set the table as part of helping get dinner ready.
Photo courtesy Sarah Jackson Photography

Parents have the opportunity to model good eating habits, and it seems to work, because children who eat with their family most nights are less likely to be overweight or obese. The entire family is likely to eat a somewhat better diet overall—more whole grains, vegetables and fruit, and fewer fats and trans-fats. This is, of course, true only if healthy meals are available; a meal with loads of fat, salt, and HFCS (high fructose corn syrup) isn't going to do much good for anyone's diet—even if it's eaten around the dining room table.

Other benefits from eating a meal together are a bit less obvious. A recent study, for example, compared kids who ate dinner with their families more than five nights a week with those who had family dinner fewer than three times a week. They found that having more family dinners correlated with a less use of tobacco, alcohol and other drugs, as well as better grades.

Another study (Harvard, 1996, Valdes) found that, for young children, eating dinner with the family was critical to language development, having more impact even than play or being read to. This effect was more pronounced in households where dinner conversation involved story-telling and long discussions rather than simple instructive comments like "eat your broccoli".

Nobody is crediting simply sitting down at the table together with all these benefits; there are surely more complex forces at work. But something positive seems to happen when parents and kids sit down at the table for a meal and conversation.

Figure 5.2
There are a lot of different tasks involved in making dinner, including taking prepared plates of food to the table.
Photo courtesy Sarah Jackson Photography

Knowing that something is good for you and your family and actually managing to do it regularly are, however, two very different things. Believe it or not, preparing dinner with your child can be relaxing and fun. Sure, you have to bring a little extra patience, but there are strategies for making dinner preparation easier. Here are a few tricks you may want to try:

▶ **Have an appetizer**—Have a small, light, healthy snack ready to go when you get home from work. Yes, this is technically a before-dinner snack and therefore suspect but if you call it an appetizer, you have transformed it into restaurant fare—and kids love restaurants! This is a great time for treats like vegetables and naturally low-fat dips like hummus or black bean salsa, although an *occasional* round of blue cheese isn't such a bad thing. You may find that your kids eat a surprising amount of vegetables they might otherwise shun. The light snack also helps with portion control at dinner since everyone won't be quite so ravenous.

▶ **Give your kids choices during preparation**—Letting your child choose between two *equally acceptable* options (which vegetable, perhaps, or what to put on a salad) while you are making dinner helps avoid fussing at the dinner table. This also gives them an incentive to help out in the kitchen. After all, they aren't there just to be your assistant and follow orders; they can help make decisions.

▶ **Plan ahead**—An hour spent planning menus for the week, and then making a shopping list for missing ingredients, will save you both time and money.

▶ **Prep tomorrow's dinner tonight**—When you have menus planned for the week, you can organize your time better, prepare ingredients for a few nights at once, and so on. This is also a good time to prepare tomorrow's appetizer so you can quickly set it out the next evening.

▶ **Make leftovers on purpose**—Double recipes and freeze half for a quick, low effort dinner on a busy night.

▶ **Look for the "Freezes Well" icon**—Recipes in this book that can be frozen and cooked or reheated include the "Freezes Well" icon to help you find them.

▶ **Develop your own routine**—Figure out what works for your family and do it regularly so both you and your kids know what to expect. Forget about how things "ought to be"—your schedule only has to work for your family. If 7:30 is when everyone can be home for dinner, then dinner at your house should probably be at 7:30. A healthy appetizer that people can snack on before dinner is particularly handy for this sort of schedule, but it can be done.

Pasta with Spring Greens and Asparagus

THIS PASTA DISH is easy to prepare and features the fresh flavors of spring. It comes from Michelle Stern, the owner of What's Cooking (www.whatscooking.info), a certified green company offering healthy cooking classes and parties to children in the San Francisco Bay Area.

Serves 4

Active Time: 15 minutes

Total Time: 30 minutes

Tools: Large pot for pasta, skillet, colander, wooden spoon or tongs, knife, and serving bowl

Nutrition per Serving: 398 Calories; 12g Fat (27.4% calories from fat); 14g Protein; 58g Carbohydrate; 3g Dietary Fiber; 17mg Cholesterol; 225mg Sodium

Ingredients

10 to 12 oz pasta, any short shape

1 pound fresh asparagus

2 tablespoons olive oil

2 to 3 cloves garlic, minced

6 to 8 ounces fresh greens, such as arugula or watercress

1/2 cup feta cheese or crumbly goat cheese

Salt and freshly ground pepper to taste

Directions

1. Heat a large pot of water for the pasta. Meanwhile, trim tough ends from the asparagus spears. (The kids can rinse the asparagus and then bend each stalk of asparagus to break off the tough ends.) Cut the spears into two-inch long pieces and set aside. When the water comes to a boil, cook the pasta according to the package directions.

2. While the pasta is cooking, heat the oil in a skillet, add the garlic and sauté over low heat for 1-2 minutes. (Kids can peel the paper skin from the garlic and mash it with the bottom of a heavy glass or small skillet.) Add the asparagus and a small amount of water, and cover and steam until the asparagus is done to your liking but still bright green. Check it after 2-3 minutes so it doesn't overcook.

3. Add the greens, cover, and steam very briefly (less than a minute will do), until wilted.

4. Combine the pasta with the asparagus and greens mixture in a serving bowl and toss well. Crumble the cheese over the pasta mixture Season with salt and pepper and serve at once.

Cook's Tip

Michelle uses fava beans and greens from the farmers market for this recipe, and loves their fresh and bright flavor.

Mary Had a Little Lamb Burger

L ACED WITH MELTED CHEESE and bits of sweet shallots, these burgers are a refreshing change from the typical burger. There are a lot of small lamb producers and grass-fed local lamb isn't much more expensive than what's available at the supermarket. Check localharvest.org for farms near you.

Makes 5 1/4 lb (pre-cooked) burgers

Active Time: 15 minutes

Total Time: 25 minutes

Tools: Mixing bowl, skillet, and spatula

Nutrition per Burger (Without Bun): 278 Calories; 20g Fat (64.8% calories from fat); 23g Protein; 1g Carbohydrate; trace Dietary Fiber; 94mg Cholesterol; 127mg Sodium

Ingredients

1 lb ground lamb

1 shallot, diced

3 ounces feta cheese (or blue cheese)

1/4 teaspoon ground pepper

1 clove garlic, minced

Bread or sandwich rolls

Cook's Tip

Many kids love smooshing the raw meat between their fingers. Just make sure they wash their hands with warm water and soap beforehand and again when they are done.

Directions

Photo courtesy FarmgirlFare.com

1. Crumble the lamb and cheese into a large bowl. Add the minced shallot, garlic, and a sprinkle of pepper. Mix well, but gently. (Any kid old enough to not eat the raw meat is old enough to help with this.)

2. Shape the burgers into four patties, gently but firmly pressing the meat together. The center of the burger always puffs up when it is cooking, so it should start out slightly depressed when you shape it. A three year-old fist makes the perfect indentation! (You can freeze prepared burgers to cook later.)

3. Place lamb patties in a cold skillet, turn on the heat to medium and cook for about five minutes, until browned. (Starting in a cold skillet minimizes shrinkage.) Flip and cook another five minutes, to desired degree of doneness.

4. Assemble your lamb burgers with your favorite condiments, fresh greens, and a slice of tomato or tart green apple.

Try This: Homemade Hamburger Buns

Homemade hamburger buns can turn a simple burger into a special meal. A recipe like the "Cheddar and Caramelized Onion Breadsticks" in Chapter 7 (page 196) gives you extra flavors that complement the lamb burger. Try making matching burgers and buns, such as heart burgers, perfect for Valentine's Day.

Lemon Rosemary Chicken

FRESH ROSEMARY AND LEMON infuse this chicken with flavor and keep it moist while cooking. Make a double batch and freeze one chicken to cook another night or cook extra for school lunches.

Serves 6

Active Time: 15 minutes

Total Time: 3 hours

Tools: Mixing bowl, whisk, small jar with lid, a large freezer bag (or other container that can hold chicken), baking sheet, and basting brush (optional blender)

Nutrition per Serving: 400 Calories; 24g Fat (53.9% calories from fat); 30g Protein; 16g Carbohydrate; 1g Dietary Fiber; 141mg Cholesterol; 504mg Sodium

Ingredients

2/3 cup fresh rosemary, chopped

1/4 cup Dijon mustard

1/4 cup honey

1/2 cup lemon juice

3/4 teaspoon salt

1/4 teaspoon ground cayenne pepper

3 tablespoons diced garlic

1 roasting chicken, cut into pieces

Directions

1. Whisk together the chopped rosemary, mustard, honey, lemon juice, garlic, salt, and cayenne in a bowl until well combined. Alternatively, leave the rosemary leaves and peeled garlic whole and toss it all into a blender on high for 10-15 seconds.

2. Pour 1/4 cup of marinade into the jar, cover, and refrigerate. Put the remaining marinade into the freezer bag, add the chicken, seal the bag, and turn it a few times so the chicken is coated. Refrigerate for two hours, turning it over a few times. (The chicken can be kept in the refrigerator overnight, or frozen for several months.)

3. Half an hour before cooking the chicken, place the bag of chicken on the counter and turn the oven on to 375°. (If the chicken is frozen, thaw it in the refrigerator—not on the counter—for 1-2 days.) Place the chicken pieces on a baking sheet. Bake for 30-40 minutes, basting with the reserved marinade a few times, until the chicken is cooked through. Serve immediately or later, at room temperature. Refrigerate leftovers once they are thoroughly cooled.

Cook's Tip

If you use a vacuum bag to hold the chicken while it marinates, the liquid will be drawn into the meat, making it moister and more flavorful.

Stuff Yourself Silly Squash

INDIVIDUAL SQUASH HALVES hold a tasty sausage mixture. You can create many variations on this dish, using a wide range of cooked grains, other (or no) meats, and adding almost any vegetable your kids like. Wild rice, which lends a nutty flavor to this dish, is available in the bulk section of many stores.

Serves 2

Active Time: 20 minutes

Total Time: 1 hour

Tools: Baking dish, saucepan, skillet, wooden spoon, and mixing bowl

Nutrition per Serving: 348 Calories; 5g Fat (13.3% calories from fat); 17g Protein; 62g Carbohydrate; 6g Dietary Fiber; 43mg Cholesterol; 590mg Sodium

Ingredients

1 Acorn squash

4 ounces bulk chicken sausage (or ground chicken)

1/2 medium onion, chopped

1/4 cup raw wild rice

1/4 cup raw brown rice

1/4 teaspoon salt

1 teaspoon chopped fresh sage (1/2 teaspoon dry)

1-2 cloves garlic, crushed

1 ounce pecans, chopped

Directions

1. Preheat oven to 350°. Bring 1 1/2 cups of water to a boil in a medium saucepan and add wild rice, brown rice, and salt. Turn heat down to low, cover and simmer until tender; about 50 minutes. Turn off the burner, uncover the rice and if there is excess liquid, drain it off. Fluff the rice with a fork.

2. While the rice is cooking, cut the squash in half from tip to stem. Run a spoon around the center of the squash, scoop out the seeds and stringy pulp, and discard. (You can also snip the pulp out with scissors.) Place the squash cut side down in baking dish with a little water, poke a few holes in each half and bake at 350° for 20-30 minutes, until a knife slides in but meets some resistance.

3. While the squash bakes, crumble the sausage into a skillet and cook on medium heat until it is browned. Add the chopped onion to the pan and cook for 2-3 minutes, until the onions are translucent. Remove the pan from the heat and drain off the fat.

4. Mix the sausage, cooked rice, sage, garlic, and pecans together in the bowl. Fill the squash with the sausage mixture, heaping it up a bit. If there is extra filling, put it in a small baking dish and heat alongside the squash. Pop the squash back in the 350° oven for 30 minutes or so to heat through.

Canadian Bacon and Cheese Soufflé

SOUFFLÉS REALLY ARE MAGICAL CREATIONS, rising above the top of a dish as they bake, and kids love to be part of the fun. Although soufflés might seem intimidating, they actually consist of simple parts—a flavored sauce base, grated cheese, maybe a little minced meat or vegetables, and a mound of stiffly-beaten egg whites. Don't open the oven while they are baking, but if you can see through the door, pull up chairs during the last few minutes so the kids can watch them rise.

Serves 4

Active Time: 30 minutes

Total Time: 1-1 1/4 hours

Tools: Saucepan, wooden spoon, whisk, mixing bowl, and *straight-sided* baking dishes: 4 1-cup ramekins or a single 1-1 1/2 quart dish. Optional, but very useful, an electric mixer

Nutrition per Serving: 305 Calories; 23g Fat (66.6% calories from fat); 16g Protein; 9g Carbohydrate; trace Dietary Fiber; 218mg Cholesterol; 660mg Sodium

Ingredients

1 teaspoon butter

1 tablespoon whole wheat bread crumbs

3 tablespoons butter

3 tablespoons all-purpose flour

3/4 cup non-fat milk

3 eggs, separated

1 egg white

1/4 teaspoon cream of tartar

3/4 cup sharp cheddar cheese, shredded

2 slices cooked Canadian bacon, chopped

1/4 teaspoon salt

1/4 teaspoon paprika

Directions

1. Preheat the oven to 375 degrees. Prepare the baking dish by buttering and then coating with breadcrumbs. Set aside.

2. Make a roux by melting the butter in a small saucepan over medium-low heat. (A roux is a cooked mixture of flour and fat that is used to thicken and add flavor to sauces.) Add the flour and continue to cook, stirring frequently, for 5-7 minutes, until bubbly but not browning. Turn down the heat, if needed, to avoid scorching.

3. Whisk the milk into the roux slowly, and continue to cook, stirring frequently, for 5-10 minutes, until very thick. Remove from the heat and scrape it into mixing bowl to cool just a bit while you beat the egg whites.

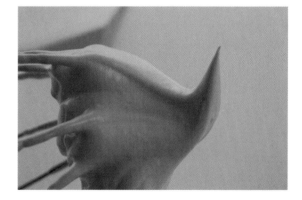

4. Put the egg whites in a mixing bowl. Beat on low speed for a minute, until the whites are frothy. Add the cream of tartar, increase speed to medium, and continue beating the egg whites until soft peaks begin to form. Increase speed to high and beat until stiff peaks form. Check your egg whites frequently so you don't overbeat them—you can see the egg whites become curdled and lumpy when they have been beaten too long.

5. Stir the egg yolks, ham, salt, and paprika into the sauce.

6. Gently fold 1/3 of the egg whites into the base to lighten the mixture. Fold in the rest of the egg whites while sprinkling in the grated cheese. (It helps to have a small child around to sprinkle things.)

7. Carefully spoon the mixture into baking dish(es); they should be no more than 3/4 full. Have a kid run a clean finger around the top edge of the dish to remove any drips (or the soufflé won't rise). Bake individual ramekins for 20 minutes, a single soufflé for 40-45, until it rises above the top of the baking dish and is browned on top. Serve immediately. The soufflés will start to deflate quickly once they are removed from the oven, so gather the family at the table just before you serve them.

Cook's Tip

A few tips for great soufflés:

▶ Make sure the sauce base is thick enough to support the rest of the ingredients.

▶ Chop meat and vegetables finely and cook them briefly before adding to base if needed to reduce excess moisture. This is particularly true for greens like spinach.

▶ Coarsely grate cheese. If it is too fine, it will clump and weigh down the whites.

▶ Don't overbeat the egg whites.

▶ A soufflé must be served immediately or it will deflate so make sure that the rest of dinner is ready, the table is set, and everyone is ready to eat when the soufflé comes out of the oven.

How to Beat Egg Whites

It is surprisingly simple to turn a few small egg whites into a huge billowy mound if you remember a few basics.

Use a deep metal or glass bowl and an electric mixer (or whisk attachment on an immersion blender) if you have one. Any significant amount of fat, like a drip of yolk, can make it impossible to whip the egg whites, so separate the eggs into two small dishes and then pour the whites into the mixing bowl after checking for stray bits of yolk.

1. Beat room temperature egg whites slowly at first, medium-low on a mixer, for about a minute, until they are frothy. Add cream of tartar, if you are using it, and increase the speed to medium-high. If you are adding sugar, add it slowly while the mixer is running. After a few minutes, the whites will double (or triple) in volume, and will become cloudy with a layer of foam on top.

2. Continue beating on medium-high and you will soon see tracks of the mixer in the egg whites. If you stop the mixer and lift the beater, the egg whites will fall in ribbons that remain visible on the surface of the egg whites.

3. Continue beating for another minute or two and soft peaks will form.

4. For stiff peaks, beat for another minute or two on high speed, checking frequently to avoid overbeaten egg whites, which are more likely to deflate while baking. Stop as soon as they hold a stiff peak, when they are smooth and glossy. Overbeaten egg whites lose their sheen and appear curdled.

Pizza Your Way

THE DOUGH FOR THE CRUST is mixed up in a few minutes and refrigerated until the next day so you can have fresh, homemade pizza in an hour! There is also a variation for two-hour pizza, in case you are in a hurry.

Makes 2 12" pizzas

Active Time: 15 minutes to make the dough, 15 minutes to assemble

Total Time: Overnight (see two-hour variation), plus 45 minutes to prepare and bake

Tools: Mixing bowl, mixing spoon, parchment paper, baking sheet or baking stone, and peel

Nutrition per Slice (1/8 of 12" pizza, crust only): 110 Calories; 2g Fat (17.6% calories from fat); 3g Protein; 19g Carbohydrate; 1g Dietary Fiber; 0mg Cholesterol; 135mg Sodium

Pepperoni and Mozzarella: 228 Calories; 12g Fat (46.9% calories from fat); 10g Protein; 21g Carbohydrate; 1g Dietary Fiber; 24mg Cholesterol; 493mg Sodium

Canadian Bacon and Pineapple: 189 Calories; 7g Fat (31.5% calories from fat); 10g Protein; 23g Carbohydrate; 2g Dietary Fiber; 20mg Cholesterol; 404mg Sodium

Classic "Everything" (Pepperoni, Sausage, Onions, Peppers, Mushrooms, Olives, Cheese): 226 Calories; 11g Fat (45.5% calories from fat); 9g Protein; 22g Carbohydrate; 2g Dietary Fiber; 24mg Cholesterol; 437mg Sodium

Ingredients

Crust

1 1/4 cups white whole wheat flour

2 cups bread flour

1 1/2 teaspoons yeast

1 1/2 cups cold water

1 teaspoon salt

2 tablespoons olive oil

1-2 tablespoons chopped fresh herbs such as rosemary, basil, or oregano (optional)

Directions

Toppings for One Pizza

1/4 cup sauce (the marinara on page 135 works well)

2-3 ounces of meat and/or vegetables, thinly sliced

2 ounces of cheese, grated or in thin slices

Cook's Tip

Parchment paper is very helpful when you are making pizza, especially if you are making more than one. You can prepare each pizza on a sheet of parchment and then slide the paper from counter to peel or cookie sheet.

1. Mix the white whole wheat flour, bread flour, yeast, salt, and herbs in a large bowl to combine. Add the water and olive oil and stir vigorously until a soft, not entirely cohesive dough forms.

2. Turn the dough out onto well-floured counter and knead for 3-4 minutes, sprinkling with more flour as needed. Place dough in a covered bowl or sealed plastic bag and put it in refrigerator overnight. (The dough can stay refrigerated for up to three days or be frozen for several months)

3. An hour before you want the pizza, turn the oven on to 500°. (If you have a baking stone, put it in the oven when you turn it on, before the oven gets hot.) At the same time, remove the dough from the refrigerator and put it on a lightly-floured counter. Divide in half for two 12" crusts. (Divide each half into 2-4 pieces for smaller or individual pizzas.) Roll each piece of dough into a ball. (The dough in this picture has flecks of chopped fresh rosemary added for extra flavor.)

4. With well-floured hands, shape each portion of dough into a flat disk as large as possible without tearing the dough. When the dough starts to shrink back immediately after stretching, let it rest on counter for five minutes before continuing with shaping it.

6. Spread a thin layer of sauce on the crust, leaving a narrow edge of the crust uncovered. Layer on the rest of the toppings, but don't overload the pizza or it will be soggy. Leave some of the meat partially exposed under the cheese, so the edges brown a little, which is both pretty and flavorful.

5. When the crust is the desired size, place it on a parchment sheet, cover, and let rise until you are ready to top it. If you turned on the oven when you took the dough out of the refrigerator, this should be another 30-45 minutes. It will not rise substantially, but it should warm to room temp and poof just a bit in spots.

7. Carefully slide pizza (still on parchment) onto the hot stone (or put cookie sheet in oven). Bake at 500° for 4-5 minutes and then check to see if the pizza needs rotating for even baking. Continue baking until cheese is melted and bottom of crust is brown and has desired crispiness; usually another 4-5 minutes, depending on how carried away you got with the toppings. Remove pizza from the oven using a peel if you have one.

Cook's Tip

Making pizza gives you a great opportunity to experiment with different combinations of toppings, many of which you might never see on a restaurant menu. If you keep a few simple rules in mind, you can throw caution to the wind and see what you create.

The first thing you put on a pizza crust is the sauce. While a thin red sauce is traditional, you might also try pesto, roasted red pepper sauce, or even a simple brush of olive oil. Venturing further afield, some restaurants feature pizzas with a sauce of pureed squash or curry so there seems little reason to rein in your imagination. Whatever you decide, the sauce should be spread in a thin layer, leaving about 1/2-1" uncovered on the edge. If you are putting fresh herbs on the pizza before it bakes, you can put them on top of the sauce.

Vegetables, which generally need to be protected from the extremely hot oven, go on next. Thinly sliced or diced is best. Sprinkle any hard cheese, like parmesan, on top of the vegetables.

Last is the cheese, and meat if you are using any. It is a good idea to leave the meat partially exposed so it will get crisp, but you also want gooey, melted cheese on top. The easiest way to accomplish this is put on half of the meat and then sprinkle about half of the cheese over the top of it. Put the rest of the meat on next and finish with the remaining cheese.

Try This:
Two-Hour Pizza

To make this dough for immediate use, make these changes to the recipe:

▶ Use warm water (about body temperature).

▶ Increase the yeast to 2 teaspoons.

▶ After kneading in step 2, place the dough in a lightly oiled bowl, cover with clean towel and let rise on the counter until doubled in size, about 1 1/2-2 hours.

▶ Turn the oven on after the dough has been rising for an hour.

Cook's Tip

This pizza crust can be frozen, raw, for up to three months, so you may want to make an extra large batch with that in mind. To freeze unbaked pizza crust, after step 3, tightly wrap each flattened piece of dough in two layers of plastic wrap. Place rounds of dough in a freezer bag and place on a flat surface in the freezer.

To thaw, unwrap a round of pizza dough and place it on a lightly floured counter for 30 minutes while the oven preheats. When the crust is thawed enough to work with, stretch it into a full size crust, put on a piece of parchment paper, and then top and bake as usual.

FREEZES WELL

Meatballs and Salsa Marinara

THIS VERSION OF THE OLD FAVORITE spaghetti and meatballs comes from The Inn at Crippen Creek Farm (crippencreek.com), where Don and Kitty Speranza's guests savor old family recipes. These meatballs, which have been in the family for over 70 years, are paired with a fast, fresh marinara. He says, "When I was a kid, I spent Saturday evenings helping my mother roll out the meatballs getting them ready to cook in the Sunday sauce." Don makes his meatballs with locally-raised, extra lean meat, but I've also included a variation with poultry and spinach for a lower-fat option.

Serves 6 (with extra meatballs)

Active Time: 40 minutes

Total Time: 60 minutes

Tools: Mixing bowl, skillet, large fork or tongs, large pot, and colander

Nutrition for Pasta and Sauce: 339 Calories; 6g Fat (14.9% calories from fat); 12g Protein; 65g Carbohydrate; 8g Dietary Fiber; 0mg Cholesterol; 196mg Sodium

Nutrition per Meatball: 180 Calories; 13g Fat (68.5% calories from fat); 11g Protein; 3g Carbohydrate; trace Dietary Fiber; 85mg Cholesterol; 294mg Sodium

Ingredients

Meatballs

1 pound lean ground beef

1/2 pound ground pork

2 cloves minced garlic

2 teaspoons dried basil

1 1/4 teaspoons salt

1/4 teaspoon black pepper

1 cup milk

1 cup fresh bread crumbs

3/4 cup grated Romano cheese

3 extra large eggs

2 tablespoons olive oil, for frying the meatballs

Pasta and Sauce

1 pound uncooked whole grain pasta

2-3 tablespoons olive oil

1 medium yellow onion, finely chopped

4 cloves fresh garlic, finely chopped

1 28-ounce can of crushed plum tomatoes

1 teaspoon of dried basil (or 4-5 leaves of fresh, finely chopped)

Salt, to taste

Freshly ground black pepper, to taste

Pinch of crushed red pepper (optional)

Directions for Meatballs

1. Put the bread crumbs in the bowl with the milk and let them soak for 5-10 minutes. Squeeze out the excess milk and discard. Return the bread crumbs to the bowl.

2. Add the ground beef, pork, cheese, spices, and eggs to the bowl. Mix thoroughly with your hands.

Try This: Meatloaf

Don says, "This mixture makes a great meat loaf. Just don't put catsup on it!"

3. Shape the mixture into balls about the size of a large egg by rolling them lightly between the palms of your hand. It's helpful to keep a bowl of warm water nearby to dip your hands in. It makes rolling the meatballs easier.

Try This: Make It Healthier!

These meatballs are so good that it's worth indulging in the original version occasionally. For a lower-fat version that's got an extra boost of vitamins, substitute chicken and/or turkey for the beef and pork, add chopped spinach and prepare as usual.

Prepare a bunch (or bag) of fresh spinach by washing it well, chopping it up just a bit, and sautéing it in a skillet with the tiniest bit of olive oil for a few minutes. This helps to cook off a lot of the water and reduces the huge pile of greens to a small handful of lovely, vitamin-packed emerald green pile. Mix in with the rest of the ingredients before shaping meatballs. (You can also use frozen spinach, but make sure it is very well drained.)

Nutrition per Meatball: 130 Calories; 8g Fat (57.7% calories from fat); 12g Protein; 2g Carbohydrate; trace Dietary Fiber; 94mg Cholesterol; 309mg Sodium

4. Heat 2-3 tablespoons of olive oil in a large skillet (cast iron, if you have it) over medium heat and brown the meatballs, turning them occasionally and carefully. They should be done in about 10 minutes. Check them occasionally, starting after about eight minutes. Cook them in batches, if needed, but don't crowd the meatballs too tightly in the pan. Put the cooked meatballs on a plate, loosely covered with foil, in a 250° oven to keep them warm while you cook the rest.

Cook's Tip

This recipe makes a lot of meatballs but Don tells us that you have to make extras because you will devour several of them before they get into the sauce. If you have leftover meatballs, freeze them (after they are cooked and thoroughly cooled). Reheat them and serve plain with a salad and some fresh whole grain bread for a simple dinner or make a meatball sandwich for lunch.

Directions for Sauce

1. While the meatballs are cooking, heat a large pot of water for the pasta. Heat a wide heavy saucepan over medium heat. Pour in the olive oil, add the chopped onion and fry, stirring frequently, for 3-4 minutes, until the onion is soft and transparent. Add the chopped garlic and continue cooking another 3-4 minutes, until the onions are beginning to brown on the edges and the garlic is fragrant. Turn down the heat if needed to avoid browning the garlic; it can become bitter if overcooked.

Cook's Tip

To use this sauce for the pizza recipe on page 128, add a teaspoon or two of water to a half cup of sauce and smooth it in a blender if desired.

2. Add the tomatoes, basil, salt, black pepper (and red pepper if using it), and cook on medium-high for about 15-20 minutes, stirring occasionally. The fast cooking helps to reduce the sauce and thicken it, but turn it down a bit if you have to so the sauce doesn't burn on the bottom.

3. When the water boils, cook the pasta until it is slightly less than done and then drain it well. Add the pasta and meatballs to the sauce and continue cooking for another couple of minutes, stirring often. (This gives the pasta extra flavor from the sauce.) Sprinkle with grated Pecorino Romano or Parmigiano Reggiano and serve immediately.

6

Sides and
Salads

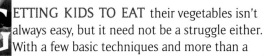

GETTING KIDS TO EAT their vegetables isn't always easy, but it need not be a struggle either. With a few basic techniques and more than a dozen recipes to get you started, your family can start to create your new favorite vegetable dishes.

Eat Your Vegetables

VEGETABLES AND FRUIT are an important part of a healthy diet and a good source of fiber, vitamins, and other nutrients. The exact number of servings recommended vary depending on whose nutritional guidelines you are reading, but everyone agrees that many kids aren't getting enough fruits and veggies.

As a general guideline, preschoolers should get 3-5 servings a day and older children from 5-7, whereas teenage boys should add a few servings to that. Everyone should be eating at least a little bit more vegetables than fruit. It is hard to get a kid to eat too many vegetables—although the same is not necessarily true for fruit—so look at these numbers as a minimum.

Each of these is considered a serving of vegetables or fruit:

▶ 1/2 cup of non-starchy, non-leafy vegetables (broccoli, beans, peas, carrots, and so on)

▶ 1 cup of raw leafy vegetables

▶ 3/4 cup of vegetable juice

▶ 1/2 cup fruit—fresh, frozen, or canned in juice

Let your children choose new vegetables when you go shopping. Walk through the produce section and find interesting new items to experiment with. If you shop at a farmers market, ask for recipe suggestions; many supermarkets even have preparation tips or recipes posted around the produce section. Every new vegetable will not be a hit, of course, but the shared exploration of new tastes is fun even when it's not a new favorite.

Figure 6.1
Many vegetables, even the humble carrot, come in an array of vibrant colors and interesting shapes and textures, making it easy to have a rainbow of colors on your plate.

When you are choosing vegetables, opt for those with bright, deep colors, they generally have more nutrients than their paler counterparts. Potatoes, for example, while not the most nutritious vegetable, are many children's vegetable of choice. By switching to sweet potatoes, you double the fiber and add a huge dose of vitamin A—more than double the recommended daily allowance (RDA)!

Texture is also an important part of how a food "tastes" and this is particularly true when it comes to vegetables. Some kids really dislike overly cooked vegetables, not because of the actual taste, but because the texture or color is unappealing. Try serving the same vegetable prepared several different ways to discover which methods your child prefers. Make sure to serve raw vegetables with dip, too. If you let kids try a variety of vegetables, and prepare them in interesting ways, they just may end up eating a surprisingly broad range of foods.

NOTE

Although they are frequently disparaged, frozen vegetables are one of the simplest and quickest vegetable options and they may even be more nutritious than their fresh counterparts. Vegetables for freezing are picked at the peak of ripeness, which is also the point of highest nutrition, and usually processed immediately. A quick blanching does reduce some of the water-soluble vitamins, like vitamin C, but the subsequent freezing locks in the rest of the nutrients. You can buy organic frozen vegetables for a reasonable price, and they are often a better flavor and nutritional bargain than that "fresh" produce that has spent the last week or two traveling across the country to reach your store.

Creative Ways To Prepare Your Veggies

Many different vegetables can be prepared using a few simple techniques. Each combination of vegetable and method produces a slightly different result. Boiled potatoes, for example, have a fairly bland taste, which is part of why folks like to pile butter on their mashed potatoes. Roast the same potatoes in a hot oven, however, and deep, sweet flavors emerge as starch is converted to sugar and caramelized. With some basic techniques and an adventurous spirit, you can make everyday vegetables interesting and more nutritious.

Steaming—Place vegetables in a pan with about 1/2" of boiling water. Cover and cook until vegetables are tender. If you have a steamer basket, place the vegetables in it rather than directly in the water.

Microwave—This method of preparing vegetables preserves the most nutrients. Place vegetables in a microwave safe bowl, add a few tablespoons of water, cover the bowl, and microwave on high for 2-4 minutes, stirring once. This method is particularly good for frozen vegetables, but also works well with fresh broccoli and cauliflower florets, and other small items, although cooking time will vary.

Sauté—Briefly cook cut vegetables in a skillet with a dollop of olive oil and a sprinkle of salt. Soft summer vegetables like squash and green beans are very good made this way, as are winter greens.

Oven-roasted—This is a simple way to coax a lot of flavor from vegetables without a lot of fuss. Wash and cut vegetables into similar sized pieces. Toss the vegetables with a little olive oil and a sprinkle of salt, adding whatever herbs and spices strike your fancy. Spread on a baking sheet and bake in a 400° oven, flipping once after 20-30 minutes. Continue to cook until vegetables are tender and starting to brown at least a little bit. Total cooking time varies, but it is generally 40-60 minutes. While roasting is often used for vegetables like potatoes, onions, carrots, and bulb fennel, it is also an excellent way to cook asparagus, summer squash, and other softer vegetables, although for a briefer time.

Sweet Potato Sticks

THIS HEALTHIER ALTERNATIVE to French fries takes less time than a trip to the local drive-through and is so much tastier! It comes from Katrina Hall, who writes about her lifelong love of food at ShesIntheKitchen.blogspot.com.

Serves 4

Active Time: 10 minutes

Total Time: 35 minutes

Tools: Vegetable peeler, knife, baking sheet, and metal spatula

Nutritional Information Per Serving: 122 Calories; 3g Fat (18.5% calories from fat); 2g Protein; 24g Carbohydrate; 3g Dietary Fiber; 0mg Cholesterol; 279mg Sodium

Ingredients

2-3 sweet potatoes (about 1-1 1/4 lbs)

2 tablespoons olive oil

1/4 teaspoon salt

Sprinkle of pepper

Directions

1. Preheat oven to 350°. Peel the sweet potato. Cut in thick slices, and then cut slices into large matchsticks.

2. Place sweet potato sticks on the baking sheet. Drizzle olive oil over the sweet potatoes and turn them in the oil so they are well coated.

3. Arrange the sweet potatoes in a single layer. Bake for about 20 minutes, until the sticks are tender when poked with a fork. Turn the heat to broil and cook for a few minutes, until some of the sticks have toasty brown spots. Be sure to watch them so they don't burn. Remove them from the oven, sprinkle with salt and pepper, and serve immediately.

Cook's Tip

Cut vegetables into different shapes with fun scissors or cookie cutters before using them. Kids can help with supervision, and it makes veggies more fun to work with!

Tex-Mex Bean Salad

SUSAN OF FARMGIRL FARE (farmgirlfare.com) makes this vibrant salad in summer when her garden is bursting with fresh vegetables, but the ingredients are available year round. Make it ahead of time for a ready-to-go side dish for potlucks and hot summer days.

Serves 8

Active Time: 20 minutes

Total Time: 20 minutes

Tools: Knife, grater, mixing bowl, and mixing spoon

Nutritional Information per Serving: 280 Calories; 5g Fat (13.8% calories from fat); 15g Protein; 48g Carbohydrate; 11g Dietary Fiber; 7mg Cholesterol; 110mg Sodium

Ingredients

Salad

1 head green cabbage, shredded (about 3 cups)

1/2 head red cabbage, shredded (about 1 cup)

2 large sweet red peppers, diced

2 medium carrots, grated

4 large scallions, chopped

1 (15-ounce) can black beans, drained and rinsed

1 (15-ounce) can whole sweet corn, drained (or 1-1/2 cups cooked fresh corn)

Salt to taste

High Kickin' Creamy Tomato Dressing

1 pound juicy tomatoes (about three medium sized), coarsely chopped

1 cup non-fat yogurt

1 cup sour cream

3 tablespoons apple cider vinegar

3 cloves garlic, peeled and chopped

1 tablespoon ground cumin

1 teaspoon ground coriander seeds

1 teaspoon chili powder (or more to taste)

1/2 teaspoon salt

Directions

1. Combine the dressing ingredients in a blender and blend until smooth. Store in a tightly covered container in the refrigerator for up to three days. Shake well before using.

2. Stir together the green cabbage, purple cabbage, red peppers, carrots, black beans, and corn in a large bowl.

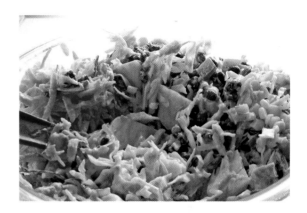

3. Add two cups dressing and mix well, adding another 1/2 cup dressing if desired. Salt to taste. Serve immediately, or for best flavor, chill for several hours or overnight. This will keep in the refrigerator for 2 to 3 days.

Try This:
Veggie Tacos

To make vegetarian tacos in a flash, spoon a generous helping of slaw into a taco shell or tortilla, and then top with fresh tomatoes, chopped cilantro, and sour cream, if desired.

Wild and Crazy Rice

S WEET BITS OF SAUTÉED ONION, pepper, and mushrooms add flavor and nutrition to a blend of wild and brown rice. This dish is low fat and high in protein, vitamin C, and niacin. Try it with the Lemon Rosemary Chicken and some Sweet and Sour Glazed Carrots for a colorful and nutritious dinner.

Serves 4

Active Time: 15 minutes

Total Time: 1 hour and 20 minutes

Tools: Knife, medium saucepan, and wooden spoon

Nutritional Information per Serving: 198 Calories; 4g Fat (14% calories from fat); 12g Protein; 37g Carbohydrate; 2g Dietary Fiber; 0mg Cholesterol; 26mg Sodium

Ingredients

1/2 medium onion, chopped

1/2 medium bell pepper, chopped

1 teaspoon olive oil

1/2 cup long-grain brown rice

1/2 cup wild rice

2 1/4 cups low-sodium chicken broth

1 cup chopped mushrooms

1/2 teaspoon thyme (fresh, if possible)

Directions

1. Heat a saucepan over medium heat for a minute. Add olive oil, onions, and pepper and cook, stirring frequently, for 3-4 minutes, until everything is sizzling and the onions start to become translucent.

2. Add brown rice and wild rice. Continue to cook, stirring often, for another 2-3 minutes, until the rice starts to smell toasty.

3. Add stock, mushrooms, and thyme. Increase the heat to high just long enough to bring to a boil, stir briefly, and then reduce the heat to low. Cover the pan and simmer, without stirring or uncovering the pot, for 50 minutes. Turn off the heat and let the pan sit, still covered, for another 15 minutes to finish steaming. Fluff the rice and serve.

Cook's Tip

Cooking time differs from one variety of rice to another so the actual length of time it takes this dish to cook may vary a little bit. The first time you make it, pay attention to cooking time and make a note in the margin if it is significantly different from the recipe.

Good Zuchs!

G REEN AND YELLOW ZUCCHINI pair up in this simple dish. Choose small zucchini, six inches in length or smaller if possible, for the best flavor and texture.

Serves 4

Active Time: 10 minutes

Total Time: 10 minutes

Tools: Knife, large skillet, and spatula

Nutritional Information per Serving: 44 Calories; 2g Fat (43.2% calories from fat); 2g Protein; 5g Carbohydrate; 2g Dietary Fiber; 0mg Cholesterol; 136mg Sodium

Ingredients

1 teaspoon olive oil

1 green zucchini

2 yellow zucchini (or crookneck squash)

1 clove garlic, minced

1 tablespoon pine nuts

1/2 teaspoon oregano

1/2 lemon, juiced (about 4-5 teaspoons)

1/4 teaspoon salt

Directions

1. Wash the zucchini and slice into 1/2" thick rounds. Heat the olive oil in a large skillet over medium-high heat. Add the zucchini and squash to the pan and cook, stirring frequently, for 2-3 minutes, until the squash begins to brown.

2. Add garlic, pine nuts, and oregano and cook for another 2-3 minutes, just until the squash is tender, but still firm. (It gets smushy and falls apart if overcooked.) Squeeze the lemon over the top and serve immediately.

Photo courtesy Sarah Jackson Photography

Sweet and Sour Copper Pennies

S WEET HONEY and tangy cider vinegar combine in this simple and versatile side dish that can be served hot, cold, or in between. These carrots take just a few minutes to make and pack a hefty dose of vitamin A.

Serves 4

Active Time: 5 minutes

Total Time: 15 minutes

Tools: Knife, saucepan, and wooden spoon

Nutritional Information per Serving: 46 Calories; 1g Fat (20.1% calories from fat); 1g Protein; 10g Carbohydrate; 3g Dietary Fiber; 3mg Cholesterol; 30mg Sodium

Ingredients

2-3 large carrots

2" piece of cinnamon stick (or a sprinkle of ground cinnamon)

1 teaspoon honey

1/2 teaspoon cider vinegar

1 teaspoon cold butter

Salt to taste

Directions

Cider vinegar has the acidic quality of white vinegar, but it is not as sharp, so it works well barely warmed, as in this recipe. The contrast to the sweet carrots is present but not overpowering. Different flavors of vinegar, and other types of acids, change the taste considerably. Experiment with them by substituting an equal amount of one of these ingredients for the vinegar:

▶ Balsamic vinegar

▶ Rice vinegar

▶ Fresh lemon juice

For a sweet version, leave out the vinegar, add a handful of chopped walnuts, and a grating of fresh nutmeg.

1. Wash the carrots and cut them into 1/2" thick rounds. Place in pan with enough water to cover them about halfway. Add a sprinkle of salt and a small piece of cinnamon stick. Simmer until tender, but not soft. Drain off most, but not quite all, of the liquid (leave about a tablespoonful).

2. Add honey and vinegar to the pan and stir the carrots to coat. Add the cold butter and stir quickly to glaze. Serve immediately or chill for up to three days.

Garlic-Braised Winter Greens

THESE TASTY COOL WEATHER GREENS take only a few minutes to prepare. You can use a single type of green, such as the rainbow chard shown in the photos, or try a mix of braising greens such as kale, beet, collard, escarole, spicy mustard, and the irresistible dinosaur kale. Look for greens at local farmers markets and most grocery stores, either in a mix or as individual items you can mix and match to make your personal blend.

Serves 4

Active Time: 10 minutes

Total Time: 10 minutes

Tools: Skillet and spatula or tongs

Nutritional Information per Serving: 18 Calories; 1g Fat (56.6% calories from fat); trace Protein; 2g Carbohydrate; trace Dietary Fiber; 0mg Cholesterol; 45mg Sodium

Ingredients

1 teaspoon olive oil

1 large bunch mixed braising greens (kale, chard, collards, and so on)

2 cloves garlic, minced

1 teaspoon fresh oregano, chopped

1/4 teaspoon red pepper flakes (optional)

Pinch of salt

Directions

1. Wash the greens and dry them by firmly holding the stems and flicking them over the sink. Discard heavy stems, except with the chard. Tear or cut the greens into bite-sized pieces. Cut the heavy center rib and stems with scissors, if needed.

2. Heat the olive oil in a skillet on medium-high heat. Add the most substantial greens, garlic, oregano, and optional pepper flakes. Cook, stirring often, for 1-2 minutes, just until the greens wilt. Add other greens in batches as described in the accompanying Cook's Tip. After you've added everything, check your greens for tenderness. You might need to add a tablespoon or so of water and cover the pan to steam the greens briefly, 1-2 minutes, until everything is tender. Serve immediately.

Cook's Tip

All greens are not created equal but you can mix whatever array of greens you have available, as long as you do it in the right order. Braising greens is not an exact science, but there are some general rules to keep in mind:

▶ Collard greens usually take the longest time, 5-7 minutes, to become meltingly tender. Chard takes about a third less time, and kale a bit less than that. In general, if you cook one type of green until it is wilted, you can add the next type and it will all balance out when it is done.

▶ Beet or radish greens, as well as salad greens like escarole, radicchio, spinach, and arugula, cook very quickly so add them when the heartier greens are almost done, after steaming

▶ Mustard and turnip leaves add a nice bite of spice to greens but can become bitter when cooked so chop them up and stir in just before you pull the greens off the heat.

Roasted Cauliflower

THIS SIMPLE METHOD of preparing cauliflower transforms the humble vegetable into something else entirely. Smooth and nutty, with crispy and caramelized edges, this is so good you may want to make extra.

Serves 2-3

Active Time: 10 minutes

Total Time: 40-60 minutes

Tools: Knife, mixing bowl, baking sheet, and aluminum foil

Nutrition per 1/3 Head: 88 Calories; 9g Fat (89.5% calories from fat); 1g Protein; 2g Carbohydrate; 1g Dietary Fiber; 0mg Cholesterol; 99mg Sodium

Ingredients

1 head cauliflower

2 tablespoons olive oil

1/8 teaspoon salt

Directions

1. Preheat oven to 425°. Remove the leaves from the cauliflower and cut off the stem level with the head. Slice the cauliflower in 1/4" thick slices.

2. Toss the cauliflower slices and olive oil in a bowl to coat well.

3. Spread the cauliflower slices on a foil-lined baking sheet and sprinkle with the salt. Bake for 30-45 minutes, until the cauliflower is well-browned. Check after 30 minutes. If the cauliflower is not done, check every 5 minutes until it is, turning the slices if needed to prevent burning.

Cook's Tip

This recipe depends on the cauliflower cooking long enough to brown and caramelize, but exactly how long that takes varies a bit depending on the moisture in the cauliflower, the thickness of slices, and so on. The first time you make this, start sampling small pieces after about 25 minutes and keep cooking until the flavor mellows, loses its overt cabbage taste, and becomes almost nutty tasting. After you make this a time or two, you will learn the right combination of size, time, and temperature for making this in your kitchen.

Nap'ple Slaw

MILD NAPA CABBAGE, tart apple, fennel's sweet licorice flavor, and a lightly tangy dressing make this versatile slaw perfect with late summer barbecues and school lunches. Served alongside a bowl of chili or soup, its light crunch offers a nice contrast to other flavors of fall. Get out the plastic knife so the kids can cut the Napa cabbage into piles of frilly shreds.

Serves 4

Active Time: 15 minutes

Total Time: 15 minutes

Tools: Knife, mixing bowl, and mixing spoon

Nutritional Information per Serving: 174 Calories; 16g Fat (75.6% calories from fat); 1g Protein; 10g Carbohydrate; 3g Dietary Fiber; 6mg Cholesterol; 135mg Sodium

Ingredients

1 fennel bulb

1 head Napa cabbage

1 Granny Smith apple

1/4 cup walnuts, broken into small pieces

1/3 cup mayonnaise

1 tablespoon lemon juice

1/2 teaspoon sugar

1 teaspoon caraway seeds

Cook's Tip

Crisp, aromatic bulb fennel is slightly sweet with a distinct licorice flavor. It is a good source of vitamin C, fiber, potassium, and manganese. Look for a relatively small, heavy, unbruised bulb with crisp, upright stalks and no flowers, which indicate an over-ripe plant. Save the stalks to use later in a sauce or soup.

Directions

1. Stir mayonnaise, lemon juice, sugar, and caraway seeds together in the mixing bowl.

2. Peel and core the apple. Chop into small cubes. Place the apple in a mixing bowl and stir to coat with dressing so the apples don't start to brown.

3. Remove the stalks from the fennel. Cut off the stem end and slice the bulb into quarters lengthwise. Slice diagonally to remove the core. Slice the fennel thinly. Add the fennel to the bowl.

4. Slice cabbage crosswise into thin strips. Add the cabbage and walnuts to the slaw and stir to combine. Serve immediately or refrigerate, covered, for up to three days.

Salsa Verde

F RESH MINT brightens up a traditional salsa verde. Serve as a dip or a fresh sauce on Mexican dishes, fish, or poultry.

Makes 2 cups

Active Time: 10 minutes

Total Time: 30 minutes

Tools: Knife, baking sheet, aluminum foil, and blender or bowl and spoon

Nutritional Information per Serving: 32 Calories; 1g Fat (16.7% calories from fat); 1g Protein; 7g Carbohydrate; 2g Dietary Fiber; 0mg Cholesterol; 137mg Sodium

Ingredients

1 pound tomatillos

2 jalapeño peppers

2-4 stems (20-30) mint leaves

1/4-1/2 cup cilantro

Juice of 1 lime (3 tablespoons)

1 medium onion, peeled and cut in 10-12 pieces

2 cloves garlic, peeled and quartered

1/2 teaspoon salt

1/4 teaspoon sugar

NOTE

To make this without a blender, chop the onions and cooled tomatillos and jalapeños, mince the garlic finely, and chop the herbs just before combining.

Directions

1. Husk and wash the tomatillos. Cut them in half and place, cut side down, on a foil-lined baking sheet.

2. Slice the jalapeños in half lengthwise, and discard the stem and seeds. Place peppers on the baking sheet, cut side down. Broil on high for 5-7 minutes, until the skin begins to char. Remove from the oven and cool for 10-15 minutes.

3. Wash the herbs by swishing them, upside down, in a deep bowl of cold water. Flick the herbs dry over the sink and pat dry with a towel. Cut off the long cilantro stems and discard them. Remove mint leaves from stems by holding the tip of the mint in one hand and running your other hand from the top of the stem to the bottom, pulling the leaves off as you go. Pinch the tips of the leaves off the stem.

4. Place tomatillos, jalapeños, onion, garlic, lime juice, mint leaves, cilantro, salt, and sugar in a food processor. Process until the salsa is of the desired smoothness. Adjust salt and herbs as needed. Refrigerate if not serving immediately. Most kids can dunk the herbs to wash them, and all but the smallest can flick a stem or two of mint without making a mess. Cilantro, however, has a lot of small stems, so make sure they can hold on tightly before you let them flick a bunch of it!

Try This: Mild Salsa

Add a mashed avocado to this salsa for a richer, somewhat milder flavor.

Sunny Spinach Salad

FOR A SPINACH SALAD that's sure to please, add some fresh orange. You can make this salad with the produce that is available in the middle of winter and it will seem almost like a sunny day.

Makes 4 servings

Active Time: 10 minutes

Total Time: 10 minutes

Tools: Salad spinner or towel, salad bowl, and large spoons or tongs

Nutritional Information per Serving: 192 Calories; 17g Fat (78.2% calories from fat); 3g Protein; 7g Carbohydrate; 2g Dietary Fiber; 7mg Cholesterol; 164mg Sodium

Ingredients

1 bunch spinach

1/2 red onion, thinly sliced

1 orange

1/4 cup pecans

3 tablespoons olive oil

1/4 teaspoon salt

1 tablespoon raspberry or other fruity vinegar

1/4 cup goat cheese, crumbled

Directions

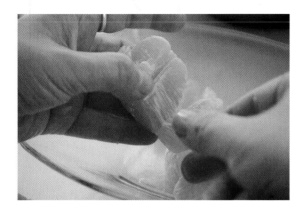

1. Wash the spinach and tear any large leaves in half. Place the spinach and onions in a salad bowl. Peel the orange, removing as much of the bitter white pith as possible. Cut the orange in half crosswise, and then break it into individual segments.

2. Drizzle the olive oil over the spinach and toss it gently to coat. Sprinkle the vinegar over the spinach and mix again.

3. Spread the onion, pecans, orange, and goat cheese on top of the spinach and serve. (If you toss it at this point, all the goodies will sink to the bottom of the bowl!)

Buy Organic When You Can!

Recent studies have compared the nutritional value of meat, milk, and eggs from grass-fed organic sources with conventional, non-organic products and found that the organic options offer a substantial nutritional advantage. They have found that organic vegetables may well have more nutrients than comparable produce grown using industrial methods. One recent study also showed that organic produce contained less lead, mercury, and aluminum than their conventional counterparts. Even though it may cost more, you might decide that it's worth it for the health of your family.

Greek Village Salad

LIKE MANY AMERICANS, I thought that a Greek salad started with a bed of romaine lettuce. Fortunately, I have friends in Athens, so I asked them what was in a Greek salad. Turns out that the traditional Village salad (which is, of course, not a "Greek salad") is a mélange of tomatoes, cucumbers, olives, and sweet peppers, topped with a chunk of feta cheese and not a bit of lettuce in sight. This, then, is the sort of salad you would get if you were in Greece, although not necessarily a "Greek salad" as Americans might think.

Serves 4

Active Time: 15 minutes

Total Time: 15 minutes

Tools: Mixing bowl and large spoon.

Nutritional Information per Serving: 140 Calories; 11g Fat (66% calories from fat); 3g Protein; 9g Carbohydrate; 2g Dietary Fiber; 13mg Cholesterol; 567mg Sodium

Ingredients

1/2 red onion, sliced into rings

2 tomatoes, sliced into wedges

1 cucumber, cut in half and then into 1/2" thick slices

6 small sweet peppers, cut into bite-sized pieces

1/2 cup kalamata olives

1 tablespoon olive oil

1/4 teaspoon salt

1/2 lemon, juiced (4-5 teaspoons)

3 ounces feta cheese

1 teaspoon fresh oregano, chopped

Directions

1. Place the onion, tomato, cucumber, pepper, and olives in a large bowl.

2. Drizzle the vegetables with olive oil and lemon juice. Sprinkle on the salt and toss the salad to coat it with dressing. Serve immediately or cover and keep at room temperature for up to several hours.

3. To serve, scoop the salad into a serving bowl, place the block of feta cheese on top of it, and sprinkle on the fresh oregano.

Cook's Tip

If small sweet peppers aren't readily available, use a bell pepper. Look for a pepper that is red, yellow, orange, or even purple if you can find it, but remember the green peppers aren't ripe yet and they do not taste as sweet.

Goin' Green Salads

MAKING GREEN SALADS a daily habit is an easy way to increase your family's vegetable consumption. A handful of greens, a few slices of carrots, and a handful of cherry tomatoes makes about one serving of vegetables, and many salads are larger than that. As a bonus, eating fresh vegetables raw is one way to ensure that you get the most possible nutrition from them.

Salads are one of the first things kids can help make. Washing vegetables, ripping up lettuce, and mixing the salad in the bowl are all simple tasks that can be done by even a small child. If your children like gardening, salad ingredients are some of the easiest plants to grow so they can make the salad from the very earliest possible point.

> **NOTE**
>
> A recent UCLA study ("A school salad bar increases frequency of fruit and vegetable consumption among children living in low-income households" Slusser, Cumberland, Browdy, Lange, and Neumann, 2006) found that students at schools with salad bars added, on average, slightly more than a serving of vegetables to their daily diet.

Use greens with a variety of textures and flavors in your salads. Remember that dark, colorful lettuce is both tastier and more nutritious. These are just some of what is commonly available:

▶ Mesclun, also called spring mix or field greens, is a varying mix of young salad greens, usually including a combination of arugula, mizuna, tatsoi, radicchio, frisse, mustard, oakleaf, red chard, and other baby leaves.

▶ Mild and tender lettuces include Boston, bibb, oakleaf, mache, and leaf lettuce.

▶ Crunch is provided by frisse, romaine, endive, and cabbage, among other choices.

▶ A number of greens are somewhat bitter, which is a nice contrast to the many sweeter salad ingredients. Try frisse, endive, radicchio, escarole, romaine, spinach, or chicory.

▶ Spicy, peppery greens include arugula, cress, mizuna, tatsoi, baby beet, and mustard greens.

Figure 6.2

Choose a variety of salad greens with different colors, flavors, and textures for an interesting and nutritious salad.

Photo courtesy FarmgirlFare.com

> **NOTE**
>
> Romaine is an exception to the "more colorful is better" rule. With 22% of the RDA of vitamin C, 29% of vitamin A, and 19% of folacin, romaine is a winner in the nutritional department.

Some herbs are also excellent in salads. Choose from anise-flavored herbs like tarragon, basil, and chervil; spicy, pungent coriander, marjoram, or oregano; peppery nasturtium; lemon balm and sour, lemon sorrel, or lemon balm; or lovage with a sweet celery taste.

Once you have selected a bed of greens, add a handful of your favorite raw vegetables. Just about any summer vegetable is fair game to be added to a salad, so pick a variety of flavors, colors, and textures. Take advantage of seasonal vegetables so your salads are always changing.

Many of the tastiest parts of a salad are best served in very small amounts. Consider things like nuts, seeds, dried fruit, olives, cheese crumbles, and other creamy and crunchy goodies. Fortunately, they generally have a reasonably long shelf life if stored properly so you can afford to parcel them out in small bits without worrying too much about spoilage.

Edible flowers are an unexpected and beautiful addition to your salad. (Make sure the flowers were grown without pesticides.) Some common garden flowers are edible—calendula, chrysanthemums, dianthus, lilacs, nasturtiums, Johnny jump-ups, pansies, and violas can go from the ornamental garden to the salad bowl. The flowers of most herbs are edible, with borage, chive, mint, sage, and thyme flowers making particularly nice additions to salads. Flowers are delicate, so scatter them on top of a salad just before serving.

Seasonal Salads

Here are a few ideas for salads that use seasonal ingredients. Every region has its own special bounty, so explore what your area has to offer.

- ▶ **Spring**—Young spinach and strawberries with a fruity vinaigrette make a simple yet very tasty salad.
- ▶ **Summer**—Leaf lettuce, mint, young carrots, crisp cucumber, and cherry tomatoes with a creamy herb dressing celebrate summer's bounty.
- ▶ **Fall**—Romaine, apple, walnut, celery, dried cranberries, and blue cheese signal the change to cooler weather.
- ▶ **Winter**—Spinach, red onion, pomegranate seeds, orange, and goat cheese use crops that are available even as we edge towards winter.

Figure 6.3
Wash lettuce by swishing it in a deep bowl of water.

To wash lettuce, fill a deep bowl with water and swish individual leaves so that any dirt falls to the bottom of the bowl (see Figure 6.3). Refill the bowl with clean water if needed. Wash spinach and crinkly lettuce thoroughly; it has lots of tiny places for dirt to hide. Dry the lettuce well in a salad spinner or by patting between two clean towels.

Cook's Tip

Containers of prewashed salad greens are convenient but can be expensive. It is easy to make your own ready-to-use mix of salad greens. Buy 2-3 heads of lettuce or bunches of salad greens, wash the whole leaves, and dry them in a salad spinner. Put the greens in a plastic bag and store in the refrigerator. Store bought lettuce should stay fresh for at least for 4-5 days, and you can easily count on twice that from produce you bought at a local farm or grew yourself.

Make Your Own Salad Bar

Most kids love salad bars, and who can blame them. All those choices. All that control. You can re-create a bit of the salad bar experience right in your own kitchen by simply serving your salad unassembled. Pile a bowl with salad greens and surround it with small bowls of other ingredients such as carrots, radishes, sweet red peppers, sliced mushrooms, and whatever other vegetables your family likes. Add a few non-vegetable options like sunflower seeds and olives and you will have your own personalized salad bar. Let the kids choose the ingredients and display them attractively for the family to choose from.

NOTE

Parents, make sure that you say please and thank your kids for helping out. Praise them in front of others on occasion, too. You might be surprised to see just how proud your kids actually are of their new skills.

Photo courtesy Sarah Jackson Photography

Presentation to Kids

Photo courtesy Sarah Jackson Photography

▶ The first thing is free: fun names! Which is more enticing: grated parmesan cheese or snow cheese!? Making up silly names for food can be very entertaining.

▶ Most restaurants put a bit of effort into making sure that food looks attractive when it is served on a plate. If you pay attention, there is often not really much involved, just a sprig of fresh herbs or artfully drizzled sauce. Look at some pictures of gorgeous and inspiring photos of food on the web and in glossy food magazines for inspiration.

▶ Cut vegetables into different shapes with cookie cutters before using them in soup or for dipping. Sandwiches can also be cut into interesting shapes—in fact, there are bread-sized sandwich cutters shaped like dinosaurs and other creatures made for just this purpose.

▶ Setting the table is another area where a little imagination can go a long way. Collect table linens, particularly napkins and placemats, which are easier to keep clean than tablecloths, so that you have a stock of colorful table settings.

▶ Washcloths make great napkins. If being absorbent, washable, and looking good when wrinkled isn't enough, they are also less expensive than many cloth napkins. Shop sales and look for baby-sized washcloths to help build your collection. Something as simple as a tying a bow around your napkins can dress up a table.

▶ Small kids enjoy doing simple craft projects like woven placemats. Cut, or tear, strips of construction paper and weave them together, then staple or glue the ends to hold the mat together. It only takes a few minutes and costs a few pennies.

▶ Look for novelty silverware and fun dishes at dollar stores, thrift shops and the like. It does not have to be high style, just bright and fun.

▶ Blow up a balloon but don't tie it. Write a name or secret message on it and let the air out. Put the balloon at each guest's place at a birthday party.

▶ Be elegant. There is no reason that kids can't enjoy a candlelit dinner with lovely instrumental music playing in the background. Bring in some cut flowers and serve everyone's drinks in wine glasses.

▶ Make a theme dinner, including food, décor, music and maybe even costumes.

Back to Basics Vinaigrette

T HIS IS A SIMPLE and classic recipe for the most basic salad dressing, requiring only vinegar, oil, salt, and pepper. The trick to a creamy vinaigrette is slowly adding the oil and mixing it in well before adding more. Once you master the creamy technique, experiment with different flavors of vinegar, oils, and herbs to create your own house favorites.

Makes 1 cup

Active Time: 5 minutes

Total Time: 5 minutes

Tools: Small bowl and whisk

Nutrition per 1/4 cup: 181 Calories; 20g Fat (98.4% calories from fat); trace Protein; 1g Carbohydrate; trace Dietary Fiber; 0mg Cholesterol; 71mg Sodium

Ingredients

1/4 cup red wine vinegar

1/2 teaspoon Dijon mustard

1/4 teaspoon salt

3/4 cup olive oil

Black pepper

1 shallot, minced

1/2 teaspoon fresh thyme, chopped

Directions

1. Whisk vinegar, mustard, salt, and pepper in bowl to combine.

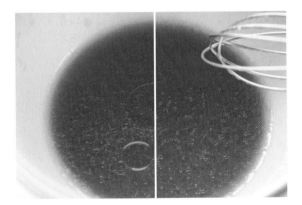

2. Pour olive oil into a small dish. Dip the whisk into the oil and then whisk the vinegar for a few seconds. Repeat 3-4 times. You should see a film of tiny oil droplets on top of the vinegar but no larger drops. If you still see larger drops, like on the left side of the image, do this a few more times—it's important to the emulsification to get this part right.

3. Slowly drizzle the rest of the oil into the vinegar while whisking. If you start to see large drops of oil, stop adding more until you whisk that in.

4. When the oil is all added and the dressing is creamy, add the shallots and thyme. Refrigerate in a covered jar if you won't be using it within a few hours. Shake or whisk before serving.

Blue Cheese Salad Dressing/Dip

SERVED AS SALAD DRESSING or dip, blue cheese is a favorite of kids and adults alike. This recipe uses non-fat yogurt to skim off a few calories without sacrificing any flavor.

Makes 1 1/2 cups

Active Time: 5 minutes

Total Time: 5 minutes

Tools: Bowl and whisk

Nutrition per 2-tablespoon (1 ounce) Serving: 70 Calories; 7g Fat (80.9% calories from fat); 2g Protein; 2g Carbohydrate; trace Dietary Fiber; 6mg Cholesterol; 200mg Sodium

Ingredients

1/4 cup low-fat milk

1/2 cup non-fat yogurt

1/3 cup mayonnaise

2 tablespoons lemon juice

3 cloves garlic, peeled and minced

1/2 teaspoon salt

1/2 cup blue cheese, crumbled

Directions

1. Whisk the mayonnaise, yogurt, milk, lemon juice, garlic, and salt together in a small bowl. Let this sit for a minute so it can thicken.

2. Stir in the crumbled blue cheese. Store, tightly covered, in the refrigerator for up to three days.

Starting a Kids Garden

Planting a special small garden with your kids can start them on a life-long adventure of growing their own food. It does not require a large space, in fact, a container is the perfect place to start. Choose a few plants—some favorite vegetables, perhaps, or a group with a single theme or common use. Here are a few ideas to get you started:

▶ **Salad garden**—Choose your child's favorite salad ingredients. You don't need a lot of space, nor to grow an entire salad. Some baby lettuce mix in a large pot or tomatoes in a hanging planter can give you that special fresh flavor you only get with home-grown produce. Look for different varieties of favorites, lettuces you never see in stores, or multicolored radishes and carrots.

▶ **Snack garden**—Vegetables that are suitable for eating straight off the vine are a good option for a child's garden, especially if that child likes vegetables and dip. Let a few sugar-snap peas climb a stake; tomatoes, baby carrots, cauliflower, and broccoli can go along with low-fat blue cheese dip for endless snacking.

▶ **Berry garden**—What could be better than a handful of berries, fresh from the bush? Berries are one of the fastest fruits to grow at home. Unlike fruit trees such as apples or pears, which take years to bear, berry bushes give fruit within at most a few years of planting. You can even find strawberry plants with berries on them at many nurseries, eliminating waiting time for impatient small people.

▶ **Plant some trash**—Even things that might be thrown away as trash when trimming produce can be grown into interesting plants. Grow a fluff of carrot fronds from a discarded top in a pot on the kitchen windowsill, or even start an avocado pit that way. Small kids particularly enjoy turning trash into plants.

Bee Yourself Honey Mustard Vinaigrette

S WEET AND TANGY, this simple vinaigrette is made with a kid-friendly method of shaking everything together in a jar. Turn on a good dancing song and make up a batch of salad dressing while you dance.

Makes 1 1/2 cups

Active Time: 5 minutes

Total Time: 5 minutes

Tools: Bowl and whisk

Nutrition per two-tablespoon (1 ounce) Serving: 70 Calories; 7g Fat (80.9% calories from fat); 2g Protein; 2g Carbohydrate; trace Dietary Fiber; 6mg Cholesterol; 200mg Sodium

Ingredients

1/4 cup fresh lemon juice

2 tablespoon honey

1 tablespoon mustard

1 clove garlic, minced

1/4 teaspoon salt

1/4 teaspoon pepper

3/4 cup olive oil

Directions

1. Place lemon juice, honey, mustard, garlic, salt and pepper into a jar with a tightly fitting lid. Close the lid securely (an adult should check for young children) and shake the jar for a few seconds to combine. Kids enjoy this step.

3. Pour the rest of the oil into the jar, replace the lid, and shake for 30-60 seconds to thoroughly mix the dressing. Store in the refrigerator if it will be more than an hour or two before using. Bring back to room temperature and shake well before serving.

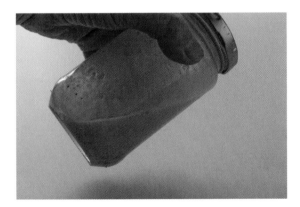

2. Add about a teaspoon of the oil to the jar. Close tightly and shake for another 10 seconds. Repeat this two more times, shaking very well each time you add oil. The oil should be broken up into tiny droplets before you add more oil.

Dreamy Creamy Herb Dressing

THE BRIGHT GREEN FLAVORS of chives and parsley make this dressing a good choice for fresh summer salads. You can add a range of other herbs in addition to these—thyme and marjoram are good choices.

Makes about 1 1/2 cups

Active Time: 4 minutes

Total Time: 10 minutes

Tools: Small mixing bowl and whisk

Nutritional Information per two-tablespoon (1 ounce) Serving: 57 Calories; 5g Fat (80.6% calories from fat); 1g Protein; 2g Carbohydrate; trace Dietary Fiber; 3mg Cholesterol; 95mg Sodium

Ingredients

1 tablespoon cider vinegar

1/2 cup low-fat milk

1/2 cup mayonnaise

1/2 cup non-fat yogurt

1-2 tablespoons Italian (flat leaf) parsley, minced

1-2 tablespoons chives, snipped into 1/8" pieces

1 clove garlic, minced

1/4 teaspoon salt

1 pinch cayenne pepper

Directions

1. Whisk the vinegar and milk together in a small bowl and let it sit for five minutes.

2. Whisk the yogurt and mayonnaise into the milk.

3. Stir in the parsley, chives, garlic, salt, and cayenne. Refrigerate tightly covered, up to 4-5 days. Shake well before using.

Photo courtesy Sarah Jackson Photography

Knead
Something!

PICTURE A BEAUTIFUL LOAF of bread; the crust, caramelized to a golden hue, hides a creamy interior. That first bite—the crackling crisp crust, slightly melting butter on still warm bread. Not much beats freshly baked bread, unless it's the tantalizing aroma coming from the kitchen while it bakes.

Good store-bought bread is, sadly, expensive and often hard to find. Learning to bake bread with your child, on the other hand, is very affordable, not to mention a heck of a lot of fun! Besides, unless you live over a bakery, there's no other way to get that "just from the oven" freshness and flavor. Or the aroma!

This chapter introduces some very useful tools. In it, you'll learn about critical ingredients and explore some techniques that you can apply to *any* recipe for better bread. A selection of recipes that accommodates the beginner baker as well as the more adventurous and experienced will give you a chance to try out your skills. Along the way, there are hints on how to adapt bread recipes to make your very own special variations.

The Basics of Bread

KIDS LOVE BAKING BREAD! They have fun exploring the organic chemistry at work—bubbling yeast, bread dough that grows, and that great moment when the rough mass smoothes into lovely, pliable dough under your fingers—and because of the need to get their hands on the dough, kids are encouraged, even *required*, to play with their food. Even better, anyone who is old enough to eat bread is old enough to help make it. Starting when they are still in high chairs, children can sprinkle flour into the mixing bowl or knead a small piece of dough—even if you discreetly throw it away after they lick it. As children get older and gain skills and confidence, they will quickly take on more of the tasks involved until they can do it all.

Bread is a pretty broad category, including treats as diverse as baguettes and blueberry muffins, cinnamon rolls and cornbread, doughnuts and...well, you get the picture. Before you start baking, let's take a moment to break this down just a bit more.

Bread is commonly divided into two big groups based on whether it contains yeast or another leavening agent (such as baking soda or baking powder). What comes to mind for most people when they think of bread is *yeasted bread*. Sandwich bread, cinnamon rolls, bagels, and baguettes are all yeasted breads. *Quick breads*, such as biscuits, coffee cakes, muffins, and scones use baking soda, baking powder, or even beer, rather than yeast, to make them rise.

Figure 7.1
Even very young children can help bake bread.
Photo courtesy Priscilla Armstrong

The choice of leavening agent also determines how bread is mixed, shaped, and baked. Yeasted breads require time to mix, knead, and let rise a time or two before baking. (Even though the process may take many hours, you can start bread in the early afternoon and have fresh bread for dinner with less than an hour of effort on your part.) Quick breads, by comparison, take far less time to mix and bake—usually well under an hour—and are often at their best still warm from the oven.

It is probably no surprise that your choice of flour can make a significant difference in how your bread turns out. Several types of flour are commonly available, each of which is best suited for a particular sort of baking. Each type of flour has a different amount of protein, which is what becomes gluten, the long strands that give yeasted bread its structure. Gluten also makes bread chewy, which is great for many yeasted breads, but not desirable for most quick breads.

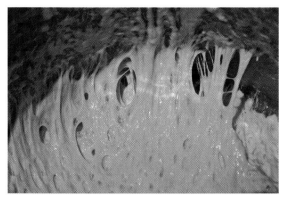

Figure 7.2
You can see the strands of gluten in this wet bread starter.

Most people have *all-purpose flour* (or *AP flour*), a white flour (made from wheat) that's fine for most baking needs. If you bake a lot of bread, however, you may want to also buy *bread flour*, which has more protein than all-purpose flour (you can approximate this effect with the addition of gluten). Cake flour, which is a soft wheat, has less gluten than AP flour, and is sometimes used to give quick breads a meltingly tender crumb.

Some flours reach near legendary status. Many Southerners swear by White Lily flour for their biscuits while bakers of artisan, rustic breads have been known to fly in flour from Europe. Fortunately, you don't have to go to such lengths to get good flour for your bread. Here are a few points to remember:

▶ **Bleached or unbleached?** Simple, unbleached is better. Bleaching removes beta-carotene, which contributes nutrition, flavor, and color to your bread.

▶ **White or whole wheat?** Whole wheat flour is more nutritious because it includes the entire wheat berry, whereas white flour contains only the endosperm (the starchy interior). Bread made with 100% whole wheat flour, however, is comparatively leaden when put up against the same recipe made with white flour.

▶ **What the heck is white whole wheat?** White whole wheat came along recently to confuse us all—it is a whole wheat flour made from a white wheat that acts more like white flour while maintaining the nutrition of whole wheat. White whole wheat is new and all of the flour made from it is not the same, so try different brands to see which you prefer.

▶ **What about other kinds of flour?** There is a world of flour out there: rye, corn, buckwheat and spelt are fairly common, but have you ever seen teff, chickpea, or amaranth flour? A trip to the bulk sections of your local food stores may yield exciting new ingredients to experiment with.

Tools and Techniques for Making Bread

A FEW INEXPENSIVE THINGS, some from unlikely sources, can make a big difference in your bread baking. Most of these tools and supplies are available at your local grocer or kitchen store. (Some of my favorite tools are available via my website at www.cookingwithyourkids.net.)

A *baking stone*, preheated with the oven, stores heat and gives it directly to the bottom of the bread for better oven spring, lighter bread and a crisp crust. A stone is absolutely indispensible for that elusive brick-oven pizza crust. Check for 1/2-3/4" thick unglazed terra cotta stones at local garden and hardware stores for an inexpensive alternative to the kitchen store version of a baking stone.

You have probably seen a *peel* at the local pizzeria. A flat piece of wood or metal is attached to a handle and used to transfer pizza and bread to and from the brick oven. If you have a baking stone, you should consider a peel to make bread baking easier.

Figure 7.3
A peel makes it easy to get bread in and out of the oven when you are using a baking stone.

Parchment paper is simply paper treated with silicone to make it less sticky when used for baking. Food sticks to the paper when initially placed on it, but when heated in the oven, the paper "releases" and the food comes right off. This paper is disposable, so unbleached is preferable to bleached, as is reusing a sheet several times before recycling or composting.

Bamboo rice paddles make excellent bread mixing spoons, especially for kids. The compact size makes them good tools when working with stiff dough. The sturdy handle is easy for small hands to grip, and the broad, almost flat surface means dough doesn't get stuck. They come in several sizes so take your children along to get the one that fits comfortably in their hands.

A *dough scraper* is used to cut and lift dough and scrape work surfaces clean. Dough scrapers are usually rectangular pieces of metal with small handles. The plastic putty knife, with no sharp edge and a bigger handle, makes a great dough scraper for children. It is available in a variety of sizes at any hardware store for under a dollar.

A handheld silicone *mini-scraper* is also very useful, particularly when mixing biscuits and other dough that needs to stay cold. These tools are sold as scrapers for dirty pans for about a dollar.

Figure 7.4
This little pan scraper is just the right size for small hands to use to mix dough.

Try This:
Replace White Flour
with Whole Wheat

Many bread recipes that call for white flour can handle 20-25% whole wheat flour and 25-50% white whole wheat flour without any further adjustment. More than that may call for an additional pinch of yeast or gluten to help compensate for the change in flour. Experiment by replacing about a quarter of the white flour with whole wheat. Increase the whole wheat until you are satisfied with the balance of texture, flavor, and nutrition.

Cook's Tip

Kids enjoy food that comes in individual servings, like rolls and breadsticks. Fortunately, you can make just about any recipe for a loaf of bread into kid-sized portions instead. To adapt a recipe, simply shape the dough as desired, let it rise (if needed), and bake at the same temperature, but for about half the indicated time. This is not an exact time, so check the bread often as it nears your estimated time. You can do this in reverse too, making a recipe for rolls into a loaf instead. Bake the loaf for about twice as long as the recipe recommends for rolls.

Cook's Tip

The most important thing to remember about quick breads is that a gentle touch matters. Wet and dry ingredients are combined and mixed quickly and lightly, to minimize gluten development. Dough is kneaded for only a few strokes and handled gently when shaping or cutting.

Exploring Yeasted Bread

YEASTED BREAD IS KITCHEN MAGIC at its finest. Simple breads, like baguettes, require just a handful of ingredients, but the transformation they undergo is pretty amazing. Sprinkle yeast and a pinch of sugar in warm water and you can watch it grow—it is alive after all! Raw flour doesn't have much flavor on its own, while salt and yeast both taste pretty bad, truth be told. Yet, if you simply add water, another relatively tasteless ingredient, you can somehow coax all that wonderful texture and flavor out of not much more than dust. Very cool stuff.

Baking bread with yeast has a rhythm of its own— and it is one that works well for children with short attention spans. You mix the dough, wait a little while, knead the dough (for less time than you think), and then can ignore the dough for an hour or two. Next, the dough gets shaped and rises again before baking. You might spend 45 minutes making bread, but it is seldom more than 10 minutes of active work at a time.

Cook's Tip

You can spread bread making out over multiple days if you need to. Refrigerate the dough in a covered container after it rises the first time, and then shape and bake within 2-3 days. (This cold fermentation trick is used by artisan bakers to improve the flavor of their bread, so your bread will taste better too!)

Figure 7.5
Sign your bread by slashing your initial in the loaf just before it goes in the oven.

Figure 7.6
This loaf of sun-dried tomato, rosemary, and pine nut bread has the large holes that characterize rustic bread and show that it was made with a high-gluten bread flour.

With a little bit of practice, you will find that homemade bread is easier than it looks. Here are a few tips to help you along the way:

▶ Always hold back one cup of flour when you are first making the dough. Mix everything else well and then add the last cup of flour a small handful at a time—or by tablespoon, if there are no small hands in your kitchen. Stop adding the flour when the dough stops absorbing it and clears the sides of the bowl.

▶ One important aspect of making yeasted bread is literally getting the feel of it right. Digging your hands into the dough tells you a number of things. Does it need more flour? Has it smoothed out?

▶ Rising times in recipes are approximations, and you should largely ignore them. What really matters is that the dough rises the amount that it is supposed to. Typically, it should double in size.

▶ Professional bakers use clear rising buckets that are marked to make it easy to see when dough has risen enough. You can approximate a rising bucket with a straight-sided container and a piece of tape. Place the tape at the level of the dough when you put it in to rise. When the dough is twice that height, it's ready.

▶ If your dough springs back when you are shaping it, let it rest a few minutes to relax the gluten. You may need to repeat the stretch-rest cycle a few times to get the dough into the desired shape.

▶ Dough rising in bread pans is ready when it appears to be almost doubled in size and feels light when you pick it up.

▶ Thumping the bottom of a loaf of bread is an easy way to test if it is done. Remove the bread from the oven, turn the bread out of the pan top down onto a clean towel in the palm of your hand, and let your child give it a thwack with their knuckles. If it sounds hollow, it's done.

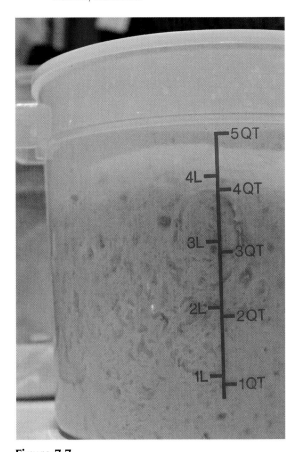

Figure 7.7

A rising bucket makes it easy to tell when your dough has doubled in size.

Coming to Terms

Autolyse (aut-oh-lees) is a short resting time that occurs after mixing the dough, but before kneading it. The flour absorbs the water and gluten starts to form so you don't have to knead as long.

Gluten gives bread the stretchy quality that helps it hold shape while it rises and, incidentally, makes bread more flavorful. Although people say that flour contains gluten, it actually doesn't. Two other proteins, *glutenin* and *gliadin*, combine to make gluten when the flour is mixed with liquid and kneaded.

Oven spring is the final burst of expansion when bread is first put in the oven. Oven spring can account for up to 15 percent of the final size of your bread. For the best oven spring (or oven kick), use a baking stone that's been preheated in the oven for 30 minutes.

Yeast is a fungus that digests some of the sugars in the bread dough and produces carbon dioxide, which is what makes the bread rise. The most commonly available forms of yeast are *instant*, which can be mixed in dough directly, and *active dry*, which must be mixed with warm water first. They are otherwise mostly interchangeable, although rising times may vary.

Cook's Tip

You can use active dry yeast instead of instant yeast in any bread recipe. Before you mix the dough, stir the yeast and a pinch of sugar into 1/2 cup of warm water and let it sit for a few minutes until it's bubbling. Add it to the dough with the rest of the liquid ingredients and mix as usual. Make sure you subtract the 1/2 cup of water from the liquid in the recipe.

Figure 7.8
It's alive! Active dry yeast added to warm water will produce bubbles to show it is alive.

Cook's Tip

If you do not have bread flour, you can make your own by adding one teaspoon of gluten flour (also called vital wheat gluten) to each cup of flour in the recipe. Mix the gluten with the flour before adding to the rest of the ingredients.

Kneading Bread Dough

Kneading bread dough distributes the ingredients thoroughly and develops the gluten so that the dough will rise and bake correctly. Even quick breads, like scones, are kneaded briefly, although sometimes only for a few strokes.

To knead bread, lay the dough on the counter in front of you. Grasp the side that is farthest away from you and fold the dough in half, towards you, as shown in Figure 7.9.

Figure 7.9
Hold the dough on the edge farthest away from you.

Using the heels of your hands, push the dough firmly away from you, as shown in Figure 7.10. Rotate the dough 1/4 turn and repeat. Quick breads usually require only a few strokes to become cohesive enough to shape, whereas yeasted dough is ready when it is smooth, supple, and no longer sticky.

Figure 7.10
Press the dough away from you.

Cook's Tip
Making Bread with a Stand Mixer

To make bread using a stand mixer, place all of the ingredients (except for one cup of flour) in the bowl and mix on low (speed 1-2) for a minute or so to combine everything. While mixing, add the last cup of flour, one spoonful at a time, stopping frequently to check how well it is being absorbed. Stop adding the flour when the dough stops absorbing it and clears the sides of the bowl. Rest dough for 20 minutes. Mix on medium for about half as long as the recipe says to knead by hand. Once the dough has smoothed out and become supple, turn it out on the counter and knead it by hand for a minute or two to finish smoothing it out.

Flaky Biscuits

B ISCUITS ARE A BREEZE to make, and having the light touch of small hands helps keep the dough tender. A small dish scraper is easy for children to hold, and lets them mix the dough without getting it warm from their hands. These are best fresh, but since they only take about half an hour from start to hot, buttery finish, that is not so hard to do.

Makes about 8 biscuits

Active Time: 10 minutes

Total Time: 30 minutes

Tools: Mixing bowl, large fork, rolling pin, baking sheet, parchment paper, round cookie cutter (or a thin-edged glass), optional food processor

Nutritional Information per Biscuit: 216 Calories; 9g Fat (37.7% calories from fat); 5g Protein; 29g Carbohydrate; 1g Dietary Fiber; 25mg Cholesterol; 923mg Sodium

Exchanges: 2 Grain (Starch); 0 Non-Fat Milk; 1 1/2 Fat; 0 Other Carbohydrates

Ingredients

2 1/4 cups all-purpose flour

3/4 teaspoon salt

1 teaspoon sugar

4 teaspoon baking powder

1/3 cup butter, cut into 1/2" squares and kept very cold

1 cup low-fat milk, very cold

Directions

1. Preheat your oven to 450°. Place the flour, salt, sugar, baking powder, and baking soda in a mixing bowl and stir to combine. Mix the butter into the flour with the fork or scraper tool until the butter is in pieces roughly the size of peas.

2. Put the flour mixture in a mixing bowl and add the cold milk. Mix together gently until just combined.

NOTE

To make these biscuits in a food processor, put all of the dry ingredients into the food processor and pulse once to combine. Add the butter and pulse 8-10 times, until the butter is in pea-sized bits. Proceed with the rest of the recipe, starting with step 3.

3. As soon as the dough holds together, turn it out on a lightly floured counter. Gently knead the dough just a few strokes until it is a mostly a cohesive ball. Your hands will warm the butter a little bit, so if you have time to chill the dough briefly after doing this, do so—your biscuits will be flakier.

4. Roll the dough into a rectangle 1/2" thick and cut into two-inch circles with a cookie cutter or glass. Place the biscuits on a parchment lined baking sheet. Bake at 450° for 8-10 minutes. Butter and eat while still warm. Gently press the dough that is left over after cutting the biscuits into a ball, wrap it in plastic, and stick it in the refrigerator for at least 30 minutes to chill it. The biscuits will be flakier than if the dough is rerolled immediately.

Savory Cheese and Scallion Scones

THESE SCONES got my good friend Susan of the award-winning Farmgirl Fare website (farmgirlfare.com) to the finals of the Pillsbury Bake Off. Luckily for me, she was happy to share the recipe. I love them with a bowl of soup in winter or a summer salad.

Makes 8 large scones (or more; see note)

Active Time: 20 minutes

Total Time: 45 minutes

Tools: Mixing bowl, small bowl, large fork or hand-sized scraper, baking sheet, parchment paper, dough scraper

Nutritional Information per Scone: 260 Calories; 10g Fat (34.5% calories from fat); 9g Protein; 33g Carbohydrate; 1g Dietary Fiber; 56mg Cholesterol; 795mg Sodium

Ingredients

2-1/2 cups all-purpose flour (plus up to 1/2 cup extra)

1 tablespoon plus 2 teaspoons baking powder

1 teaspoon salt

4 ounces feta cheese, crumbled

4 ounces cream cheese, very soft (30 minutes on the counter or 30 seconds in the microwave)

4 scallions (green onions), chopped

1 egg

1 cup low-fat milk

Directions

1. Preheat your oven to 400°. Put the flour, baking powder, and salt in a mixing bowl and stir briefly to combine.

2. Add cheeses and scallions and stir to distribute everything.

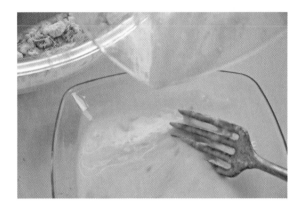

3. Break the egg into a small bowl and whisk for a few seconds to scramble it. The egg will mix with the milk better if you do. Add the milk and mix briefly.

4. Pour the egg and milk into the mixing bowl and combine the mixture quickly to form a rough dough. Sometimes the dough is very wet and you may need some of that extra 1/2 cup of flour to make it come together. Sprinkle a scant tablespoon in, mix a few strokes, and then add another spoon at a time until the dough comes together in a rough ball.

5. Turn the dough out onto a lightly floured counter and knead it a few gentle strokes. It will come together into a smooth dough very quickly and it will be tough if you over-knead it, so be gentle.

7. Transfer the wedges to the parchment-lined baking sheet using the dough scraper as a spatula.

6. Pat the dough into a circle, about 9" across and 3/4" inch thick. Cut into eight wedges with a dough scraper.

8. Bake for 20-25 minutes, until golden brown. Remove them from oven to a rack and let them cool for at least 10-15 minutes before eating.

NOTE

These scones are hearty and fairly large, so if you have small children (or light appetites) you might want to make them smaller. Divide the dough in half after kneading and form two smaller and slightly thinner rounds. Cut each of them into 6-8 wedges, depending on how large you want the scones to be. Bake for a little less time; about 15-20 minutes.

Pita Pocket Bread

PITA BREAD PUFFS UP into little balls in the oven. When the bread cools, slice it in half and stuff with your favorite sandwich fillings.

Makes 8 large or 12 small pita breads

Active Time: 40 minutes

Total Time: 2 hours

Tools: Mixing bowl, large spoon, rolling pin, clean towel, and pizza stone or aluminum foil

Nutritional Information Per Serving:

8 Pitas per Serving: 210 Calories; 4g Fat (17.2% calories from fat); 6g Protein; 38g Carbohydrate; 3g Dietary Fiber; 0mg Cholesterol; 403mg Sodium

12 Pitas per Serving: 140 Calories; 3g Fat (17.2% calories from fat); 4g Protein; 25g Carbohydrate; 2g Dietary Fiber; 0mg Cholesterol; 269mg Sodium

Ingredients

1 1/4 cups whole wheat flour

2 cups all-purpose flour

2 teaspoons yeast

1 1/2 teaspoons salt

2 tablespoons olive oil

1 1/4 cups warm water

Directions

1. Combine the whole wheat flour, one cup all-purpose flour, yeast, and salt in a mixing bowl and stir to blend.

2. Add the water and olive oil to the bowl and mix for a minute to moisten all of the ingredients. Sprinkle in the last cup of bread flour, one tablespoon at a time, and stop when the dough stops absorbing the flour. Mix for several minutes more, until the dough clears the sides of the bowl. (As always, you may need to add a little more flour.)

3. Knead on a lightly floured counter for 8-10 minutes, adding the rest of the last cup of flour, until the dough is smooth, yet still fairly soft. Cover and let rest on the counter for 30 minutes.

4. Turn the oven on to 450° (with a pizza stone) or 500° (without a stone). Divide the dough in half. Flatten each piece of dough into a 6" disk.

CAUTION

Remember the oven is extremely hot and these pitas bake very quickly, so you will have to move fast. Make sure small people stay a safe distance from where you will be juggling big balls of steam-filled bread.

5. Cut each piece of dough into four or six wedges, depending on which size pita bread you want to make.

6. Roll each piece of dough into a ball and then flatten into a disk with your hand. Cover the rounds with a damp towel and let them rest for 20 minutes.

Cook's Tip

If some of your pitas don't puff, don't despair; it seems there is a stubborn one in every batch. Make it into pita chips. Have the kids brush a pita with olive oil, sprinkle on some garlic and salt, slice into wedges, and put them on a baking sheet. Pop them into a 425° oven for a few minutes to crisp up a bit.

7. Roll each piece of dough into a very thin circle (1/8-3/16"). Small ones will be about 5" while large is about 8". Make sure you get it thin enough. If your pita is too thick, it won't puff up. Let rest for 10 minutes before starting baking.

8. Place each pita on a piece of foil directly on the oven rack and bake 5-8 minutes, until they puff up like a ball. They should not get brown

If you are baking the bread on a stone, lay as many pieces as will fit directly on the stone. If you have a spray bottle of water, spritz the bread lightly and close the oven door quickly. The bread will take only about three minutes to bake, so watch it carefully.

Remove from oven and cool on rack. Wrap bread as soon as it is cool—in a towel if you're serving it within few hours—otherwise, store it in a plastic bag.

Rosemary Fans

THESE ROLLS BLOOM in the oven into charming little fans, each with its own look. The bread dough is simple to make and shaping the rolls is quick, easy and, as you can see, not an exact science. You can substitute almost any other savory herb for rosemary, although fresh herbs really do work best.

Makes 12 large rolls

Active Time: 40 minutes

Total Time: 4 hours

Tools: Mixing bowl, mixing spoon, muffin tin, dough scraper (or knife), and pastry brush

Nutritional Information per Serving: 252 Calories; 7g Fat (23.7% calories from fat); 7g Protein; 41g Carbohydrate; 2g Dietary Fiber; 0mg Cholesterol; 536mg Sodium

Ingredients

1 1/2 cups water

1 tablespoon instant yeast

1 cup whole wheat flour

4 cups bread flour

2 tablespoons olive oil

1 tablespoon salt

1 tablespoon rosemary fresh, chopped

3 tablespoons olive oil

Directions

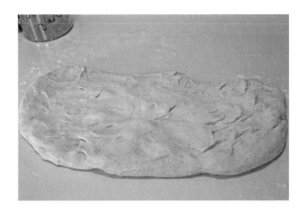

1. Put the water, yeast, whole wheat flour, three cups of the bread flour, and the olive oil in a large mixing bowl and stir to combine. Sprinkle in the last cup of flour while mixing, stopping when the dough clears the bowl (stops sticking to the sides) and stops absorbing flour. Cover the bowl and let the dough rest for 20 minutes.

3. When the dough has doubled in size, turn it out on a lightly floured counter and flatten into a rectangle with your hands. Let the dough relax for a minute while you prepare a muffin tin by lightly rubbing each cup with olive oil.

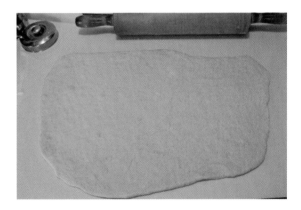

2. Turn the dough out on a well floured counter and sprinkle the salt on it. Knead the dough 10-12 minutes, until it is firm yet supple and smooth. As always, remember that you may need to add a bit more flour. Place the dough in a clean bowl and cover it with a damp cloth. Let rise until doubled in bulk (about an hour).

4. Using a rolling pin, roll the dough into a 12×18 rectangle. If the dough starts resisting and springing back, let it rest for five minutes and then finish rolling.

5. Brush the dough with olive oil and sprinkle liberally with chopped rosemary.

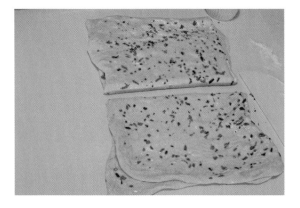

6. Cut dough in half crosswise and lay one piece of dough on top of the other. Cut that stack in half.

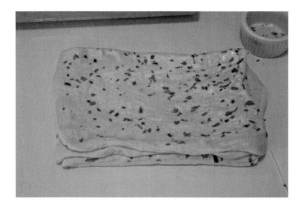

7. Place one of the pieces of dough on top of the other so that you have a single four-layer stack that's about 6×9 inches in size.

8. Cut the stack into thirds and then cut each of those pieces into four rolls. It doesn't matter if the sides are uneven, like the outside edges you see here.

9. Place the stacks in oiled muffin tins, one stack per cup with a cut edge facing up. Cover and let rise until doubled in bulk; about an hour.

10. Bake in a preheated 425° oven for 25 minutes or until golden brown. Cool rolls in pans for 10 minutes and then put them on a rack to finish cooling.

Photo Courtesy Sarah Jackson Photography

Cheddar and Caramelized Onion Breadsticks

J UST THE RIGHT SIZE for small hands, breadsticks are a big hit with kids. With sharp cheddar cheese and bits of sweet browned onions, these are sure to disappear quickly.

Makes 40-50 breadsticks

Active Time: 1 hour

Total Time: 5-6 hours

Tools: Mixing bowl, mixing spoon, parchment paper, baking sheet, and dough scraper (or knife)

Nutritional Information per Breadstick: 79 Calories; 2g Fat (17.4% calories from fat); 2g Protein; 14g Carbohydrate; trace Dietary Fiber; 3mg Cholesterol; 108mg Sodium

Ingredients

1 large onion, diced

1 tablespoon olive oil

4 teaspoons instant yeast

1 1/2 cup warm water

6 cups bread flour

1 cup low-fat milk

1/4 cup butter, softened

2 cups shredded cheddar cheese

2 teaspoon salt

Directions

1. Heat the milk in a small saucepan over medium heat, stirring occasionally, for 2-3 minutes, to scald it. Remove the milk from the heat as soon as the surface begins to shimmy, and do not let it boil. (You can also heat the milk to just under a boil in the microwave if you prefer.) Add the butter and set it aside to cool.

2. Chop the onions into small pieces. Heat a frying pan over medium heat. Pour in enough olive oil to barely coat the bottom of the pan. Add the onions and sauté for 5-10 minutes, until they start to become translucent and are brown and crispy around the edges. Scrape the onions and oil into a bowl and set aside to cool.

TIP

Cooking the onion accomplishes two things. First, it changes the flavor, mellowing it and bringing out a sweeter and more complex onion taste. The amount of water in the onions is also reduced significantly (see Figure 7.11), creating tasty little bits rather than relatively large, wet onion pieces.

Figure 7.11
Cooking the onions reduces them in size as they mellow and sweeten.

Try This:
Flavor Changes

Experiment with other hard and semi-soft cheeses such as Swiss cheese or even blue cheese. You can use bits of roasted garlic or chopped olives instead of onions, each providing a different sort of flavor.

3. Combine the water, yeast, and two cups of bread flour in a bowl and mix for about one minute, just enough to make a wet, lumpy dough. Set aside to rest until the milk is cool.

4. Add the cooled milk/butter, onions, and cheese to the mixing bowl along with three more cups of flour. Mix well, adding the last cup of flour a bit at a time until a soft dough forms. Cover the bowl and let the dough rest for 20 minutes.

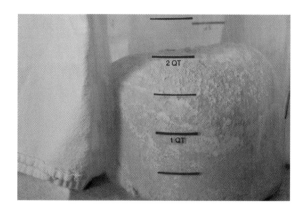

5. Turn the dough out onto a well floured counter, flatten it a bit, and sprinkle on the salt. Knead by hand for 7-10 minutes. The dough should be smooth and elastic. Place dough in clean bowl, cover, and let rise until it's doubled in bulk; about 90 minutes.

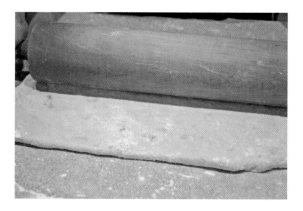

6. Divide dough in half, and set aside one piece. Shape the dough into a 9"×18" rectangle, first by hand and then using a rolling pin. Stop and let the dough rest for a few minutes when it starts springing back.

7. Cut dough into 3/4" wide strips using the dough scraper. (A pizza cutter works well too and kids who are old enough to use them like driving the little wheel around.)

8. Place breadsticks on a parchment-lined baking sheet. You can twist them if you like—or even spell your child's name if you are feeling adventurous! Cover and let rise until doubled in size; about 60 minutes.

9. Preheat oven to 350°. Bake for 15 minutes. The breadsticks should be golden brown, but still soft. They crisp up a bit as they cool and are best within a couple hours of baking.

Cook's Tip

If you don't have enough baking sheets for all of the breadsticks, cut pieces of parchment and lay them on a counter or table. Shape the breadsticks and lay them on the sheets of parchment to rise. When you are ready to bake, transfer the sheets of parchment to baking sheets or use a peel to move them to your baking stone.

Snap 'Em Up Snack Crackers

T HESE CRUNCHY CRACKERS are fun to make and you can vary the ingredients to change the flavor. After the dough is rolled out as paper-thin as possible, turn the kids loose with various seeds for sprinkling.

Makes about 60 crackers (approx. 3" square; this is a rough estimate and may vary wildly depending on how thick you roll them out)

Active Time: 30-45 minutes

Total Time: 2 hours

Tools: Mixing bowl, mixing spoon, rolling pin or pasta machine, parchment paper, baking sheet, and small knife to score crackers (need not be sharp)

Nutritional Information per 3" Square Cracker: 36 Calories; 1g Fat (37.1% calories from fat); 1g Protein; 5g Carbohydrate; trace Dietary Fiber; trace Cholesterol; 36mg Sodium

Ingredients

1 1/2 cups all-purpose flour

3/4 cup bread flour

1/2 cup rye flour

1/4 cup cornmeal

3/4 teaspoon instant yeast

1 teaspoon salt

2 tablespoons fresh rosemary, chopped

2 tablespoons fresh sage, chopped

6 tablespoons olive oil

1/3 cup low-fat milk

1/2 cup cool water, plus additional as needed

For topping:

Olive oil

Poppy seeds, sesame seeds, and/or sea salt if desired

Directions

1. Combine the dry ingredients and herbs in a bowl and stir to combine

2. Mix the oil, water, and milk in a small bowl. Add to bowl and mix until a rough, sticky, and stiff dough comes together. You may have to drizzle in a little water, a teaspoon at a time, to get the right texture. It might also be easier to mix with your hands than with a spoon.

3. Turn dough out onto lightly floured counter and knead briefly. Cover and let rest for about an hour.

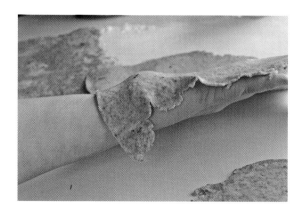

4. Preheat the oven to 350°, with a baking stone if you have one. Flatten dough by hand on lightly floured surface. Divide in half and roll into large rectangles, about 10"×18". Cut each of those rectangles in half and continue rolling the dough until it is very thin. You really can't get this dough too thin when rolling it by hand.

5. Place each sheet of dough on a piece of parchment paper. Brush the dough with olive oil and sprinkle with seeds or kosher salt if desired.

NOTE

For really thin crackers, you can roll these out with a pasta machine. In step 4, flatten the dough by hand on a lightly floured surface and divide into four pieces. Flatten each piece of dough into a 3" wide rectangle that will fit into your pasta machine (you may want the rolling pin for this) and then let the dough rest for 10 minutes. Set your pasta machine for the thickest setting and roll each piece of dough through the pasta machine once. Set the pasta machine to the next thinnest setting and repeat rolling each piece of dough in turn. Repeat until the crackers are thin enough.

---

6. Score the sheet of dough with a pizza cutter or knife. This makes it easy to break the crackers once they are done. Bake the crackers on a hot stone for 8-10 minutes, until they just start to brown on the edges. If you don't have a baking stone, use a baking sheet and bake them for an extra minute or two. In either case, the edges will brown faster and they go from done to overdone fairly quickly, so keep an eye on the first batch to determine the specific cooking time in your oven.

8

Sweets
and Treats

PICTURE YOUR CHILD BEAMING with pride as she serves her friends cookies that she made. Even better, imagine that those cookies are made from a recipe that you created together to your kid's exacting standards. This chapter ends with a discussion of how to do exactly that—make a personalized cookie with your child.

Along the way, there are recipes for everyday goodies like cookies and a simple stovetop pudding as well as a wonderfully rich chocolate mint cake that would be welcome at any party.

The Case for Cookies...

S WEETS HAVE GOTTEN A BAD RAP over the years as reasonable quantities of homemade goodies gave way to oversized, chemical and fat-laden commercial sweets. But really, there is not anything inherently wrong with the ingredients that go into many of these dishes. And I have that on the authority of a doctor...

Many years ago, I encountered my obstetrician as he was eating breakfast with two of his glowingly healthy children. You might expect that breakfast would be healthful whole grains with a bit of fruit for sweetness; at least I would have. The reality was that they were eating cheesecake. Cheesecake! 9:00 in the morning and the person I took medical advice from was letting his children eat dessert. For breakfast. Somewhat shocked, I confronted him about this nutritional gaffe. His response, "It's got eggs, low-fat cream cheese, graham crackers, not too much sugar, fresh fruit, and they are splitting a slice. I bet it's healthier than half the cereal in the grocery store!"

Although I am not recommending that you feed your children dessert for breakfast, I do think that there is a nugget of wisdom in there. If you start with real food and serve small portions, dessert is not so bad. And he's right, many breakfast cereals are pretty dreadful.

Like cereal and most other prepared food, commercially produced baked goods are all too often laden with HFCS (high fructose corn syrup) and transfats, neither of which is desirable. Yet, if you don't

Figure 8.1
Cheesecake isn't the best breakfast in the world, but it's not the worst either.

let the kids eat anything sweet, they are likely to see it as some horrible deprivation. So indulge your family in the occasional treat; just do it wisely.

For example, this chapter includes a seriously rich chocolate cake, made with butter and a cake-sized dose of sugar. It is also cut into 16 slices, rather than the usual 12. Portion control strikes again. You should not eat this, or any, cake every week. When you do have a slice of cake, however, it should be worth the time it takes to make it and the calories you consume while eating it. Trans-fats and artificial flavors are not worth it; but moist, rich chocolate cake with mint filling is.

Pay attention to portions. Most people will finish off the entire serving of whatever if it is put in front of them, so make sure that you put reasonable portions on the table. It will not feel like deprivation to have a small piece of pie if the pie is fresh and tasty. The first few bites of any food seem to be what counts the most, anyway. Think of the first cherries of summer or a piece of good chocolate when you have not had one for quite a while. One small cookie is often just enough to stave off the desire to stuff your head in the cookie jar.

Don't overlook the power of presentation. Dress up simple food into an enticing dessert that delights your child's eyes before they even start eating. Here are a few suggestions:

▶ **Several tiny balls of ice cream are much cuter than a single, larger scoop.** A two teaspoon cookie scoop turns a 1/2 cup serving of ice cream into eight small balls, which looks like a lot more than a single half-cup scoop.

Figure 8.2
These two dishes have the same amount of ice cream in them, even though they don't look like it.

▶ **Sprinkles are not just for decorating cookies.** A few candy sprinkles on a plate can turn an otherwise plain dessert festive.

Figure 8.3
Make even simple desserts attractive to your kids.

▶ **Serve a plate of tiny treats.** One very small cookie, some sliced fresh fruit, and a small square of chocolate provide three contrasting tastes and textures without a lot of fat or sugar.

▶ **Cut fruit with small cookie cutters.** Watermelon stars are much more fun than plain old slices.

▶ **Ice cream is a treat on its own, but a very small scoop can transform a piece of fruit into dessert while adding very few calories or fat.**

Craisy Nutty Brownies

FREEZES WELL

THESE RICH, MOIST BROWNIES, full of dried cranberries, pecans, and chocolate chips, are simple to make yet special enough to stand out at a party.

Makes one 9×13 pan (64 brownies)

Active Time: 10 minutes

Total Time: 35 minutes

Tools: 9×13 pan, microwave safe mixing bowl, and mixing spoon

Nutritional information per 1" x 1 1/2" Bar: 77 Calories; 5g Fat (56.8% calories from fat); 1g Protein; 8g Carbohydrate; 1g Dietary Fiber; 18mg Cholesterol; 38mg Sodium

Ingredients

6 ounces unsweetened chocolate

3/4 cup (1 1/2 sticks) butter

1 1/2 cups sugar

4 eggs, room temperature

1 teaspoon vanilla extract

1 cup white whole wheat flour

1/2 teaspoon baking powder

1/4 teaspoon cinnamon

1/4 teaspoon salt

1 cup dried cranberries

3/4 cup chopped pecans

1/2 cup semisweet chocolate chips

Directions

1. Preheat oven to 375°. Butter and flour a 9×13 pan and set it aside. Place chocolate and butter into a microwave safe mixing bowl and heat in microwave at medium (50%) power for 60-90 seconds, stopping to stir a few times, until the chocolate is mostly melted. Remove from microwave and stir until the chocolate is completely melted.

3. Combine white whole wheat flour, all-purpose flour, salt, baking powder, and cinnamon in a small bowl. Gently stir into chocolate mixture until there are only a few visible streaks of flour. Add dried cranberries, nuts, and chips and then stir until just combined.

2. Stir in the sugar, mixing well so the sugar is incorporated and starts to melt. The mixture should be cooled down to a bit above body temperature by then (you can tell by the temperature of the bowl); if not, let it cool for a few minutes. Mix in the vanilla extract and eggs, one at a time, and beat well after each one. Kids can break each egg into a small bowl and check for shells before adding to the batter.

4. Pour into prepared pan and smooth top. Bake 20-25 min. Check the brownies at about 20 minutes by shaking the pan gently. If the center jiggles, continue to bake, checking every 3-4 minutes. Brownies are done when a toothpick inserted in center has some crumbs clinging to it; inserted at the edges it does not. Cool completely in pan before cutting. These brownies keep for 3-4 days tightly wrapped on the counter; they also freeze well.

Amaretti

THESE DELIGHTFUL ITALIAN ALMOND COOKIES have a crisp, crunchy exterior and a flavorful, chewy interior. Buy ground almonds, often labeled as almond meal, at natural food stores or grind your own in a food processor.

Makes three dozen cookies

Active Time: 20 minutes

Total Time: 2 hours

Tools: Electric beater or whisk, mixing bowl, mixing spoon, zester or microplane, baking sheet, parchment paper, cookie scoop, metal spatula, and wire cooling rack

Nutritional Information per Cookie: 43 Calories; 2g Fat (36.8% calories from fat); 1g Protein; 6g Carbohydrate; trace Dietary Fiber; 0mg Cholesterol; 4mg Sodium

Ingredients

1 tablespoon all-purpose flour

1/2 teaspoon cinnamon

2/3 cup sugar, divided

1 teaspoon orange rind, grated

1 cup almonds, ground (measure after grinding)

2 egg whites

1/3 cup powdered sugar

Directions

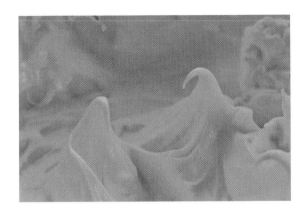

1. Whip egg whites with 1/3 cup of sugar to stiff peaks. (For tips on beating egg whites, see page 127.)

2. Stir 1/3 cup of sugar, flour, cinnamon, orange zest, and ground almonds together in a mixing bowl. Fold in the egg whites until a thick, wet dough forms.

3. Using a two-teaspoon cookie scoop (or your hands, rubbed with a few drops of vegetable oil), drop the balls of dough on the parchment lined cookie sheets. This is a great job for kids; all that oily, gooey dough is fun to play with! The cookies will spread during baking, so leave some room between them. Let the cookies rest, uncovered, on the counter, for an hour.

4. Preheat oven to 350°. Sift the powdered sugar over the cookies. Bake the cookies for 15-20 minutes, until they are puffed and lightly browned. Remove cookies from the oven and cool on a wire rack.

Ginger Applesauce Cake

NOT TOO SWEET, with a blend of warm spices and bits of nuts and candied ginger, this cake is wonderful still warm from the oven. A small scoop of ice cream on the side transforms this simple cake into a rich dessert and provides a creamy balance to the ginger.

Makes 16 yummy servings

Active Time: 15 minutes

Total Time: 45 minutes

Tools: 9" square pan, mixing bowl, electric mixer, or wooden spoon

Nutritional Information per Serving: 191 Calories; 10g Fat (45.9% calories from fat); 4g Protein; 23g Carbohydrate; 1g Dietary Fiber; 39mg Cholesterol; 197mg Sodium

Ingredients

1/2 cup butter

1/2 cup sugar

2 eggs

1/4 cup maple syrup

1 1/4 cup unsweetened applesauce

1 1/4 cup all-purpose flour

3/4 cup rolled oats

1 teaspoon baking powder

3/4 teaspoon salt

1 teaspoon ground cinnamon

1/2 teaspoon ground nutmeg

1/4 teaspoon ground ginger

1/4 teaspoon ground cloves

3/4 cup walnuts, coarsely chopped

Powdered sugar for sprinkling

Directions

1. Preheat the oven to 350°. Grease a 9" square pan. Stir flour, oats, baking powder, salt, cinnamon, nutmeg, ginger, and cloves together in a bowl and set aside.

2. Cream butter and sugar together until well combined. Add the eggs one at a time, mixing on low speed to combine. Once the eggs are incorporated, beat the mixture on high for 3-4 minutes, until it is about double in volume. (You can do this by hand, although it won't be quite as lofty. Beat vigorously for 3-4 minutes, trading off between bakers if you have more than one assistant in the kitchen.) With mixer on medium, slowly pour in maple syrup and mix in thoroughly.

3. With the mixing spoon, gently mix in the applesauce in two parts, alternating with the dry ingredients. When the mixture is just starting to come together, have your child sprinkle in the nuts and ginger while you stir a few more strokes, just until all flour streaks disappear.

4. Pour into the prepared pan and smooth the surface. Bake for 30 minutes, until a toothpick inserted in the center comes out dry. Let cool and sprinkle with powdered sugar.

Rhubarb Gingerberry Crisp

THIS SIMPLE CRISP pairs sweet raspberries with the more astringent rhubarb, resulting in a delightful dish that can be assembled quickly. Pop it into the oven when you sit down for dinner and you'll have warm crisp for dessert. Although rhubarb is actually a vegetable, it is generally used as if it were fruit in desserts, particularly in pies.

Serves 6-8

Active Time: 15 minutes

Total Time: 50 minutes

Tools: Mixing bowl, small bowl, spatula, large fork, and baking dish

Nutritional Information per Serving: 294 Calories; 11g Fat (32.8% calories from fat); 3g Protein; 48g Carbohydrate; 4g Dietary Fiber; 28mg Cholesterol; 120mg Sodium

Ingredients

1 1/2 pounds rhubarb

1/2 cup raspberries, thawed

1/2 cup brown sugar, packed

1 tablespoon candied ginger, minced

2 teaspoons arrowroot (or 1 tablespoon cornstarch)

1/3 cup whole wheat flour

2/3 cup oat flour (see page 52 to make oat flour)

1/3 cup butter

1/2 cup brown sugar

1/4 teaspoon cinnamon

Directions

1. Preheat oven to 375°. Prepare the rhubarb by trimming off the ends, stripping off the stringy outside layer (if desired), and cutting the stalks into 1" pieces. (The leaves are poisonous and should be thrown away!)

2. Stir the brown sugar and arrowroot together in a mixing bowl. Add the chopped rhubarb, raspberries, minced ginger, and then stir until well combined.

3. Mix the whole wheat flour, oat flour, brown sugar, and cinnamon in a small bowl. Add the butter and cut it in with a fork until the mixture is crumbly. You can also rub the mixture gently between your fingers to mix the butter in. (It's another chance for the kids to play with their food!)

4. Pour the rhubarb mixture in the baking dish. Sprinkle the crumb topping over the rhubarb. Bake 30-35 minutes, until bubbly and nicely browned. This is particularly good with a small dollop of whipped cream or vanilla ice cream.

Marcella's Pie Cookies

THESE COOKIES ARE the cupcake of pies: tender sour cream pastry and a rich date filling shaped into tiny little puffed flowers. Kids love rolling out the dough and filling the cookies. This recipe has been handed down in our family for about 100 years and is almost always made in double or triple batches.

Makes 30 cookies

Active Time: 40 minutes

Total Time: 2 hours

Tools: Small saucepan, wooden spoon, or silicone spatula, rolling pin, 2 1/2" round cookie cutter, baking sheet, parchment paper, metal spatula, and wire cooling rack

Nutritional Information per Cookie: 222 Calories; 7g Fat (28.4% calories from fat); 3g Protein; 37g Carbohydrate; 1g Dietary Fiber; 32mg Cholesterol; 95mg Sodium

Ingredients

8 ounces dates, chopped

2 tablespoons sugar

1 cup (2 sticks) butter

2 cups sugar

2 eggs

1 cup sour cream

2 teaspoons vanilla extract

1/4 teaspoon nutmeg, ground

1/4 teaspoon salt

5 cups all-purpose flour

2 tablespoons sugar, for sprinkling

Directions

1. To make the filling, place the dates in a saucepan with enough water to just cover them. Stir in the sugar. Simmer over medium heat, stirring frequently, about 20 minutes, until the mixture is thick enough to hold its shape on a spoon. Watch it carefully towards the end of cooking, stirring more often and reducing the heat if needed to avoid scorching. Set the filling aside to cool completely before making the cookies.

2. Cream the butter, sugar, eggs, vanilla, and sour cream. Add three cups of flour, nutmeg, and salt and mix until just combined. Spread the remaining two cups of flour on the counter and turn the dough out on top of it. Knead quickly and gently, working in the flour, to form a smooth soft dough. Refrigerate the dough at least 15-30 minutes before rolling it out.

3. Preheat oven to 350°. Working with half of the dough at a time, roll it 1/4 inch thick and cut it into two-inch rounds. (You can use other roundish shapes, as long as there is enough space in the center for the filling.) You should get about 30 rounds per half batch of dough.

4. Place half of the rounds on parchment-lined cookie sheets. Divide the cooled filling between the cookie bottoms, using a scant teaspoon per cookie. Top with another round, pressing the edges well to seal them, and sprinkle the top with sugar (use vanilla sugar if you have it). Bake 20 minutes until they are lightly browned and the crust firms up somewhat. Allow them to cool on a rack for at least 15 minutes before eating; the center is very hot!

Strawberry Ice Cream

THIS ICE CREAM has the richness that comes from using egg yolks, but without the hassle of cooking a custard base. Instead, the egg yolks are beaten over hot tap water while the milk, cream, and sugar are brought to the barest of a boil. When they are combined, the egg yolks are fully cooked in mere moments.

Makes 1 1/2 quarts

Active Time: 25 minutes

Total Time: 4 hours

Tools: Mixing bowl, large bowl (large enough to hold the mixing bowl), whisk, saucepan, strainer, rubber spatula, kitchen towel, and ice cream freezer

Nutritional Information per 1/2 Cup Serving: 190 Calories; 10g Fat (47.5% calories from fat); 3g Protein; 22g Carbohydrate; 1g Dietary Fiber; 101mg Cholesterol; 39mg Sodium

Ingredients

2 1/2 cups milk

1 1/2 cups cream

1 cup sugar

4 egg yolks

1 pint strawberries (or other fruit)

Directions

1. Put the milk, cream, and sugar in a heavy saucepan and place on medium-low heat, stirring occasionally, while you prepare the egg yolks.

2. Run tap water until it is hot and then fill the larger bowl about halfway, so that the smaller bowl will float in it. Fold the kitchen towel in half and put it on the counter next to the bowl. Place the egg yolks in the smaller mixing bowl and whisk briefly. Float the mixing bowl in the hot water (hold the edge of the bowl to stabilize it) while continuing to whisk the yolks for a minute or so, until they are frothy and warm (just under body temperature—check with a thermometer or a very clean fingertip). If it will float without tipping, leave the bowl floating in the hot water, otherwise put it on the towel.

3. Turn up the heat under the saucepan to medium-high and bring the mixture just to a boil, stirring often so it does not scorch. Place the mixing bowl on a kitchen towel so it does not slip and slowly pour the milk mixture into the warmed yolks, whisking constantly. This is a two-person job; an adult can pour the milk while the child whisks the eggs. Continue whisking for one minute after everything is combined to fully cook the egg yolks. Strain the mixture into a container, cover tightly, and chill thoroughly, preferably overnight.

4. After the ice cream base has cooled almost to room temperature, clean and chop the berries and combine them with 1/4 cup of sugar in a small bowl. Give a kid a large fork to mash the berries a bit, and then let the berries sit on the counter for 30 minutes to get juicy.

5. Crush the strawberries into a puree using a blender, immersion blender or a large fork— another great job for kids. Make sure the fruit is thoroughly mashed; large chunks of fruit will freeze hard as a rock! Stir into ice cream base and let chill for at least one hour.

6. Once the ice cream base is thoroughly chilled, freeze the ice cream according to your ice cream maker's instructions. When the ice cream is done, either serve immediately or place in a freezer-safe container and place in your freezer. Homemade ice cream does not keep as well as store-bought because it does not have all those preservatives, so eat it within a couple of weeks.

Cook's Tip

An ice water bath will cool the ice cream base more quickly. Fill the larger bowl with ice and water and float the mixing bowl in it. Remember to make sure it is stable so it doesn't tip over! The ice cream base will cool in 30-60 minutes.

Try This: Ice Cream Flavors

Instead of the strawberries, try one of these variations or create your own flavor.

Chocolate Ice Cream: Add 3-4 ounces of melted unsweetened chocolate to the hot mixture after combining. You can also use melted bittersweet chocolate bars, which gives you a broad range of flavors to choose from, but you will probably want to reduce the sugar in the recipe by 1/4-1/2 cup, depending on the sweetness of the chocolate. Leave the strawberries in for ice cream that tastes like chocolate covered strawberries!

Nutella Swirl Ice Cream: Add 1 teaspoon of vanilla to cooled ice cream base before freezing. Mix 3/4 cup of Nutella with two tablespoons of a neutral flavored vegetable oil together until smooth and softened. When the ice cream is done, pour it into the mixture and let it churn for just a few seconds—mix it too long and you will have Nutella Ice Cream instead of swirls of Nutella in vanilla ice cream. (Many ice cream machines have an opening to allow this; if yours does not, you can quickly swirl it in when you transfer the ice cream to another container after it is churned.)

Brown Sugar Ice Cream: For a light butterscotch flavor, try brown sugar instead of white. This is particularly good in the Nutella swirl and goes well with ice cream to be served with apple pie.

NOTE

You can select from quite a range of ice cream machines these days, so you are sure to find one that meets your needs and budget:

▶ At one end of the spectrum is the old-fashioned wooden bucket filled with ice and rock salt and a hand-crank, which can often be found for little to nothing at a thrift shop. Try Freecycle (freecycle.org) or Craig's List (CraigsList.org).

▶ If you prefer a more hands-off approach, you can purchase an automatic model with its own freezer for about $100.00 if you shop around a bit. Other ice cream machines require that you pre-freeze the bowl, so you have to plan ahead or store the bowl in the freezer (if you have space) so it is always ready to use.

▶ The bright red ball shown in the photograph is actually an ingenious ice cream maker that runs on human power. The ice cream base goes into a cylinder in the center from one end, while a mixture of rock salt and ice goes in the other end. After half an hour of rolling the ball around, the kids can eat the frozen treats of their labor.

Figure 8.4
The Play and Freeze makes ice cream while it's rolled around.

Butterscotch Pudding

RICH AND CREAMY butterscotch pudding is a childhood favorite. Serve this quick and tasty pudding as simple comfort food or dress it up with a dollop of whipped cream.

Makes five 1/2 cup servings

Active Time: 15 minutes

Total Time: 1 hour, or less if you like warm pudding

Tools: Small bowl, medium saucepan, whisk, wooden spoon or silicone spatula, and plastic wrap

Nutritional Information per Serving: 175 Calories; 7g Fat (35.7% calories from fat); 6g Protein; 22g Carbohydrate; trace Dietary Fiber; 131mg Cholesterol; 128mg Sodium

Ingredients

1 egg yolk

2 eggs

2 cups low-fat milk

2 tablespoons cornstarch

1 pinch salt

1/3 cup brown sugar, packed

1/4 teaspoon vanilla extract

1 tablespoon butter

Directions

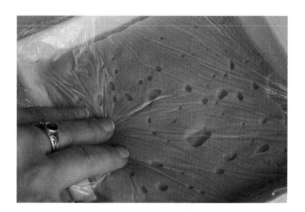

1. Lightly beat the eggs and yolk in a small bowl to break them up (as if for scrambled eggs). Whisk in the milk. Stir the brown sugar, corn starch, and salt together in a saucepan. Whisk in the eggs and milk.

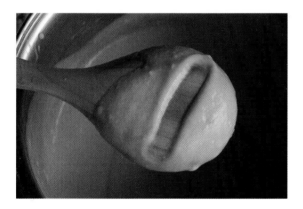

2. Heat mixture over medium-low, stirring occasionally, until the outside of the pan is warm to the touch. Turn the heat up to medium and continue to cook, stirring frequently, until it is thick enough to coat the back of a spoon. (Run your finger over the spoon; if it leaves a clear trail, it's done.)

3. Remove from heat, and then stir in the vanilla extract and butter. Pour into a bowl and cover with plastic wrap, pressing it down onto the surface of the pudding to prevent a skin from forming. If you like the skin, skip this. Let the pudding cool to room temperature on the counter. Check it frequently and place it in the refrigerator as soon as it cools.

Minty Cool Chocolate Cake

THIS INDULGENTLY RICH chocolate cake, with a hidden layer of mint frosting, is perfect for a birthday party. It takes a little time to make and frost a cake, so you may want to bake the cake one day and freeze the tightly wrapped, unfrosted cake layers. Thaw the cake, still wrapped, for just 30 minutes before frosting. (Frosting a half-frozen cake is a trick bakers use to make it easier.)

Makes 16 slices

Active Time: 45 minutes

Total Time: 3 hours

Tools: Two 8" round cake pans, two small heatproof bowls (or coffee mugs), mixing bowl, electric mixer or mixing spoon, rubber spatula, two wire cooling racks, and icing spatula

Nutritional Information per Serving: 403 Calories; 21g Fat (45.9% calories from fat); 3g Protein; 54g Carbohydrate; 1g Dietary Fiber; 78mg Cholesterol; 320mg Sodium

Ingredients

Cake

1/2 cup cocoa

1/2 cup boiling water

2/3 cup strong mint tea, cooled (brew with a generous handful of fresh leaves or 2-3 bags of mint tea)

3/4 cup (1 1/2 sticks) butter, softened

1 1/4 cups sugar

2 eggs, room temperature

1 1/2 cups all-purpose flour

1/2 teaspoon baking soda

1/2 teaspoon salt

Frosting

1 cup (2 sticks) butter

1 pound powdered sugar

1/4 cup cream or milk

1/8 teaspoon mint extract

1/4 cup cocoa

Directions for Cake

1. Preheat oven to 300°. Butter and flour two 8" round cake pans. Brew a cup of mint tea, letting it steep 15 minutes. Combine the cocoa and boiling water in a bowl and stir well to disperse the cocoa. Measure 2/3 cup of the mint tea into the bowl with the cocoa and stir until well combined. Set aside to cool.

2. Beat the butter and sugar together in a mixing bowl, on medium speed, for 3-4 minutes, until the mixture is fluffy and light (in both color and texture). Scrape down the sides of the bowl occasionally so everything gets well mixed.

3. Add the eggs, one at a time, mixing well after each addition. Your child can crack one egg into a small bowl and pour it into the batter while it is being beaten. Once the egg is incorporated, repeat with the other egg. (Adding ingredients slowly helps keep the batter from curdling.)

4. Sift together the flour, baking soda, and salt. Add to the batter in thirds, alternating with the cocoa mint tea.

5. Divide the batter evenly between the prepared pans and smooth the tops. Bake for 30-35 minutes, until a toothpick inserted into the center comes out clean. Cool the cake layers in the pans for 15 minutes, and then invert onto cake racks to finish cooling. Let the cake cool completely before frosting.

Directions for Frosting

The frosting for this cake is mixed together at first, and then divided and flavored with either mint or chocolate.

1. Beat the butter in a mixing bowl (on medium speed if you're using an electric mixer) until light and fluffy.

2. Add the powdered sugar about a cup at a time, mixing well after each addition. Add the cream gradually and mix until smooth.

3. Measure 3/4 cup of frosting into a small bowl. Measure the mint extract into a container and add it to the frosting, a few drops at a time, until you like the mint flavor. It is easy to go overboard and end up with a medicinal taste, so do this slowly!

4. Beat the cocoa into the remainder of the frosting until smooth and creamy. (Frosting can be frozen in a tightly closed container. Thaw in the refrigerator for 24 hours and stir to smooth before using.)

Frosting the Cake

For best results, frost the cake the same day you intend to serve it.

1. Place the bottom layer of cake on the serving plate. Slide small pieces of clean paper under the edges of the cake so the frosting smears onto it as you frost. Spread the mint frosting over the cake, leaving 1/2" at the edge bare. (The frosting will squish down and fill the edge when you put the other layer on.)

2. Place the second layer on top of the first, with the smoother side up. Spread about a third of the chocolate frosting evenly over the top of the cake.

3. Frost the sides by picking up a blob of frosting on the spatula and running it around the side of the cake in a smooth motion. Get more frosting when it becomes too thin to cover well.

4. Spread the remaining frosting on the top of the cake and make decorative swirls with the spatula. (This is much easier than getting a perfectly smooth surface!) When the frosting has had a chance to set, 30 minutes or so, carefully slide the paper out from under the edges of the cake.

Mini-Pavlovas

THIS ETHEREAL COMBINATION of meringue, whipped cream, and fruit was created as a tribute to the Russian ballerina Anna Pavlova and is said to resemble her tulle tutu. In Australia and New Zealand, where it originates, it is often made as one large meringue and served at Christmas dinner. In northern climates, like the US, it's a delightful alternative to summer strawberry shortcake.

Makes 6 servings

Active Time: 20 minutes

Total Time: 4 hours

Tools: Mixing bowl, electric beater or whisk, baking sheet, parchment paper, large spoon, and medium bowl

Nutritional Information per Serving: 199 Calories; 8g Fat (33.2% calories from fat); 2g Protein; 32g Carbohydrate; 1g Dietary Fiber; 27mg Cholesterol; 58mg Sodium

Ingredients

3 egg whites, room temperature

1/4 teaspoon cream of tartar

Pinch of salt

3/4 cup granulated sugar

1 teaspoon vanilla extract

1 teaspoon fresh lemon juice

1 pint strawberries

1 tablespoon sugar

1/2 cup heavy cream

Try This:
Pavlovas Your Way

You can make a Pavlova with just about any kind of fresh fruit. Nectarines and blueberries make a wonderful combination, as is a mix of in-season berries.

Lavender complements berries particularly well, because it adds just a hint of floral spice to balance the berries' sweetness. If you have lavender sugar (see page 53), you can make the meringues with it.

Directions

Making the Meringue

1. Preheat oven to 200° and line a baking sheet with parchment paper. Beat the egg whites, cream of tartar, and pinch of salt in a mixing bowl on low for 30 seconds, just enough to make the egg whites a bit foamy. Continue to beat, increasing speed gradually until the whites are thick and starting to form soft peaks. Sprinkle 3/4 cup of sugar in gradually, and then drizzle in the lemon juice and vanilla extract. Beat until the whites form stiff, glossy peaks. (See page 127 for tips on beating egg whites.)

2. Using a large spoon, make six mounds of meringue on the parchment-lined baking sheet. (This is where you decide how large a "serving" is, so make the meringues smaller if you prefer.) Flatten each mound to form a slightly concave top so the berries and whipped cream have somewhere to rest. Bake at 200° for about two hours, and then turn the oven off and let them sit in the closed oven for about 2 hours to finish drying out. You can store these in an airtight container for 2-3 days.

Making the Pavlovas

1. Slice the berries, put them in a small bowl, and sprinkle them with 1 tablespoon sugar. Cover and let sit at room temperature for 30 minutes.

2. Beat the cream just until stiff peaks begin to form. Place a meringue on a plate, and then pile with berries and whipped cream. Serve immediately so they don't get soggy.

bethCookies

STUDDED WITH CHOCOLATE CHIPS and macadamias, along with a generous helping of oatmeal and a little coconut, these are my signature cookies. This recipe makes a large batch, enough for a party, but they freeze beautifully.

Makes 5 dozen cookies

Active Time: 30 minutes

Total Time: 1 1/4 hours

Tools: Mixing bowl, mixing spoon, baking sheet, parchment paper, metal spatula, and wire cooling rack

Nutritional Information per Serving: 124 Calories; 8g Fat (52.9% calories from fat); 2g Protein; 14g Carbohydrate; 1g Dietary Fiber; 15mg Cholesterol; 77mg Sodium

Ingredients

1 cup butter

1/2 cup sugar

1 cup brown sugar

2 large eggs

1 teaspoon vanilla extract

1 1/2 cups all-purpose flour

1/2 teaspoon salt

1 teaspoon baking soda

2 cups chocolate chips

2 cups rolled oats

1 cup coconut flakes

1 cup macadamia nuts, chopped

Directions

1. Preheat oven to 375°. Beat the butter, sugar, and brown sugar until well combined. Add vanilla and then eggs, one at a time, beating until well blended after each addition.

3. Add the oatmeal, chocolate chips, coconut, and nuts and continue mixing until everything is well distributed.

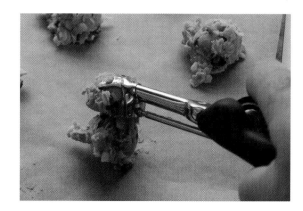

2. Combine flour, baking soda, and salt. Add to butter mixture and beat until the flour is mostly incorporated.

4. Using a two-teaspoon cookie scoop, drop the cookies on a parchment-lined (or greased) cookie sheet, leaving space for the cookies to spread. Bake for 12-15 minutes, until golden brown. Cool on a rack, and then store in tightly sealed container or freeze.

Creating a Personal Cookie

I HAVE HAD THE JOY of cooking with many small people over the years and we almost always get around to baking cookies. On more than a few occasions, the cookies come first. Our "house rules" dictate that kids get to pick which kind of cookies we bake—at least most of the time.

Sitting together on the couch flipping through cookbooks is always great fun. Some kids have a definite favorite right off the bat; they love chocolate chip cookies and while you may get them to experiment with nuts, that's about it for them. Others meander from peanut butter cookie to brownie to lemon bar and back again, unable to alight on a single choice. Those are the most fun. They are also the kids who inspired me to start making personalized cookies for people.

It's easier than you think to help your children make their very own cookies. It's also an awful lot of fun. Here's how to do it.

Start by asking your child to think about the perfect cookie. One with all of the things they like best rolled up into their absolutely favorite cookie ever. Some kids like to have cookbooks to look at, whereas others prefer to rummage through the pantry for inspiration.

There are two major aspects to consider when dreaming up your personal cookie:

▶ **Texture**—Is it crumbly, crunchy, thin and crisp, thick and chewy, or something else entirely? Is it all one mixture or are there layers, like in Jessica's Jam Bars, described later in this chapter? Are there crunchy bits, like nuts?

▶ **Flavors**—What sorts of flavors does it have? It might be chocolate, butter, brown sugar, coconut, fruit (sweet or tart?), and so on. This is where looking through the things in the kitchen in useful. Don't forget the spice rack and herb garden for mint, lemon verbena, lavender, and more.

Once you have a clue about what you want to end up with, look at recipes that resemble your desired results in overall texture (thick or thin, crisp or chewy, layered or not). It is easy to change the flavor of a cookie, but making a bar, like a brownie, into a drop cookie, like a chocolate chip, is much harder. Pick a recipe that seems like a good starting place. Don't agonize too much over the first choice, it's only a batch of cookies and even failed experiments are usually tasty.

Because you will be making similar recipes at least a few times while experimenting, you might want to make a smaller quantity until you get it right. Once you select your starting point recipe, calculate the size of a "testing batch." The easiest way to do this is to divide the quantities of the ingredients by the number of eggs in the recipe. If a recipe calls for two eggs, one cup of butter, and one and a half cups of sugar, you'd use one egg, a half cup of butter, and three-fourths cup of sugar. When you decide on a recipe, multiply ingredient quantities by the original number of eggs to have a regular sized recipe.

You can make some substitutions without much concern about how it will change the resulting cookies: walnuts to almonds, vanilla extract to lemon, white sugar to brown, or add small quantities of solid add-ins like coconut. The flavor might get odd, but the texture should not suffer much.

Other changes, however, require more work. Substituting honey for white sugar, for example, changes the moisture balance and requires other adjustments—reducing the other liquids in this case.

Make only one or two changes to the recipe at a time. That way if you really like a change, or really don't, you know what it is that made the difference. If you change several things at once, it is much harder to tease out to the actual cause and effect.

Write down the recipe each time you try a new version, *as you do it*. It's easy to change the quantities of ingredients on the fly but re-creating what you did is difficult without notes.

When you have your recipe, make sure you give it a good name. Many of my creations are simply named after the person for whom they were made, but there's no reason you can't get more creative.

Here are a few personal cookies, and the stories of how they came about, to give you a bit of inspiration.

bethCookies

bethCookies started out as oatmeal cookie recipe that a friend, Nora, scribbled in the back of my grandmother's cookbook four decades ago. The thin, crispy-chewy oatmeal cookies were great, but I am a serious chocolate fan, so I often threw in chocolate chips and other goodies that I had on hand. Over the years, this became my signature cookie, which always amused me because it wasn't until a few years ago that I started doing the same thing every time (well, most of the time) and actually wrote down a recipe.

> Thin, crisp-edged oatmeal cookie
>
> + chocolate chips
> + macadamia nuts
> + coconut
> _____
> = bethCookies

TashiaDoodles

Tashia has been baking cookies since she was a small child and invented her own cookie a few years ago. Here's her description of how TashiaDoodles came about.

TashiaDoodles started out as snickerdoodles from the Better Homes and Gardens "New Cook Book," and ran into a couple of accidents along the way. I was baking cookies in a rush as a surprise for my sister, and she always likes extra cinnamon in her snickerdoodles. When laying out my ingredients, I accidentally grabbed the nutmeg instead of the cinnamon, and almond extract instead of vanilla. Along the line I discovered my mistake, and added the cinnamon and vanilla to the dough. The clove was integrated later. Even though it started as a mistake, people love the cookie, and it has become the cookie I'm known for.

Figure 8.5
Snickerdoodles got a lot of added spice to become TashiaDoodles.

Firm, crisp, slightly chewy snickerdoodle

+ almond extract
+ cinnamon
+ nutmeg
+ cloves

TashiaDoodles

barbCookies

This is a variation of bethCookies created for a friend who is allergic to chocolate. I swapped out the chocolate chips for an assortment of chopped, dried fruit and changed the type of nuts.

bethCookies

− macadamia nuts
− chocolate chips
+ walnuts
+ almonds
+ dried apricots
+ dried pineapple

= barbCookies

Jessica's Jam Bars

These jam bars are, truth be told, a work in progress. My good friend Jessica enjoys jam bars quite a bit and I've been working on the perfect mix of cookie, fruit, and crumbly, crunchy topping. First, a thin layer of buttery shortbread is pressed into a pan. Next comes a generous layer of thick jam; homemade blueberry and raspberry are excellent. The top layer is a mix of oatmeal, nuts, flour, butter, brown sugar, cinnamon, and other spices— sort of a streusel with extras thrown in. The spices and nuts change depending on the flavor of jam being used. Raspberry, almonds, and vanilla is an excellent combination, as is blueberry, walnuts, and lavender.

Shortbread cookie
+ jam
+ oatmeal
+ chopped nuts
+ streusel topping

= Jessica's Jam Bars

Index

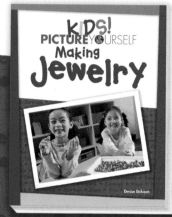

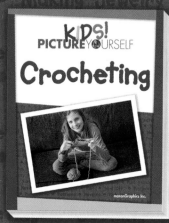